The Two Roses Way

Peter Billington
Eric Slater
Bill Greenwood
Clive Edwards

Published by Sigma Leisure – an imprint of
Sigma Press, 1 South Oak Lane, Wilmslow, Cheshire SK9 6AR, England.

British Library Cataloguing in Publication Data
A CIP record for this book is available from the British Library.

ISBN: 1-85058-338-2

Typesetting and Design by: Sigma Press, Wilmslow, Cheshire.

Maps by: Peter Billington

Text photographs: the authors

Cover: Orbit Design

Printed by: Manchester Free Press

General Disclaimer

Whilst every effort has been made to ensure that the information given in this book is correct, neither the publisher nor the author accept any responsibility for any inaccuracy.

FOREWORD

As a politician you are offered honorary titles in various bodies. As politely as possible I turn down such invitations, but made an exception when invited to become the honorary president of my local Ramblers' Association. My own rambling was influenced and guided by Ken Slater and his co-authors.

This book brings together many themes which ramblers will recognise and cherish. For many it will be a closer geographical exploration of the familiar; the beautiful border country of Lancashire and Yorkshire. It is a border which moved in 1974 when local government reorganisation took areas which I had known as Yorkshire into Lancashire, and remains, for some, disputed territory.

If the book additionally opens up that area for visitors and ramblers beyond this will be a double bonus, for the area is a little known jewel.

The book is also a gentle social and historical exploration of the area. An exploration of the countryside is not simply a question of which stiles lead to which paths. This ramble along the Lancashire and Yorkshire border opens a thousand insights, clues and starting points for the history of our country. There is nothing as redolent of our history as the title of this walk itself, "The Two Roses".

The main underlying motif of the book is one which all ramblers cherish – that of companionship. It is the joy of exploring an area in the company of friends. The conversations about that week's politics, the exchange of information about things passed on the way and the curiosity which leads you to the reference book when you get home to check just exactly the background of such and such a family, such and such an event.

The instigator of this walk, Ken Slater, and his friends and family who completed his work, embodied all these characteristics. Apart from the joys of the fresh air, particularly invigorating for Ken as a skilled engineering worker from industrial Lancashire, walking was a political act for Ken Slater and his like. His rambling was part of knowing who you are, understanding your location in time and space. Knowledge of your surroundings was not only essential to be effective politically but was a liberation; and walking the hills, taking the fresh air was actual, physical liberation.

The paramount theme of the book is the joy of knowledge shared. The countryside for Ken Slater was not a private place, and that is why so many share his determination to press for responsible access to our common heritage. The sign "Keep out!" is an offence to the idea of a world held in common.

This book is a tribute to Ken Slater. It communicates his modesty and generosity in the joy of discovering the world in which we live and act.

Michael Hindley.

Member of the European Parliament for Lancashire East. September 1992.

Contents

An Outline of the Route

An Introduction to The Two Roses Way

The Track leading up to Apronfull Hill (1,258') on the way to the Summit of Pendle Hill, on the first section of The Two Roses Way

How to Use this Guide

The map is a continuous strip (covering 71 pages of the book) on a scale of 5 inches to a mile and is read from the bottom to the top of each page. As a consequence, north is not necessarily at the top of the page and a north arrow is shown on each part of the map to indicate the correct geographical alignment. The symbols used on the map are explained in the map key and follow those used by Wainwright in his pioneering walking guides. Although the maps show all the detail necessary to walk the route they should be used in conjunction with the appropriate Ordnance Survey 1:50,000 sheet. The text accompanying each section of the walk provides details of local wildlife, geology, history, farming and topography. The 'Additional Information' (page 43) lists sources of accommodation and useful addresses.

Route Description

The Two Roses Way is a 100-mile circular hill walk through Lancashire and Yorkshire. The route begins and ends in Whalley, Lancashire, and is described in an anti-clockwise direction. The route uses rights of way throughout its length and also provides the opportunity to use the Fair Snape Fell and Embsay Moor Access Areas, when these areas are open to the public. Points on the route include: Pendle Hill, Weets Hill, Cracoe Fell, Linton, Malham, Attermire Scar, Settle, Gisburn Forest, Slaidburn, Dunsop Fell, Middle Knoll, Whin Fell, Langden valley, Fair Snape Fell, Parlick Pike, Chipping, Longridge Fell, Hurst Green, Whalley.

Maps Needed

The route can be walked using the following Ordnance Survey 1:50,000 Landranger Series maps: Sheet 103 Blackburn & Burnley, Sheet 102

Preston & Blackpool, Sheet 98 Wensleydale & Wharfedale, Sheet 104 Leeds & Bradford (2 miles only).

For those who want greater detail, the following 1:25,000 Ordnance Survey maps cover the route: Pathfinder Series SD 63/73, SD 84/94, SD 65/75, SD 44/54, SD 64/74; Outdoor Leisure Map No. 10, Yorkshire Dales (Southern Area).

Route Outline

For convenience of description, the route is divided into six sections.

1. Whalley to Gisburn – 15 miles: Clerk Hill, Wiswell Moor, track to Nick of Pendle, Apronfull Hill, Spence Moor, Barley village, Black Moss reservoirs, footpath over Rimington Moor, Howgill, Gazegill, Eel Beck Farm, Westby Hall, Gisburn.

2. Gisburn to Skipton – 16 miles: Moor Laithe Farm, Coal Pit Lane, Weets Hill, Weets House, Star Hall, Pasture Head Farm, Whitemoor Reservoir, Hey hamlet, Copy House, road to Lothersdale village, bridleway to Tow Top Farm, footpath over Ramshaw Moor, lane to Skipton.

3. Skipton to Malham – 18 miles: minor road to Embsay village, lane to Embsay Reservoir, Crookrise Crag Top, Rylstone Fell, Cracoe Fell, Peters Crag, Ravens Nest Crags, Thorpe hamlet, road and footpath to Linton village, footpath and track to Lainger House, Weets Top, lane to Malham.

If the Embsay Moor Access Area is closed, the following alternative route is used as far as Linton: Skipton, Rough Haw and Sharp Haw, Rylstone, Cracoe village, Linton. The alternative route is equal in distance to the main route. A map of the alternative route is given in the Appendix at the end of this book.

4. Malham to Slaidburn – 19 miles: Beck Hall cottage, Pikedaw Hill, Stockdale Farm, footpath to Settle, footpath beside River Ribble, footpath and lane to Gisburn Forest, Halsteads Farm, St James Chapel, lane to Black House Farm, Hammerton Hall, footpath to River Hodder and Slaidburn.

5. Slaidburn to Chipping – 18 miles: road to Burn Side cottage, Burn Fell, Whitendale valley, Middle Knoll, Brennand Farm, Whin Fell, Trough House, road and track to Langden Castle, Fiendsdale, Holme House Fell, Fair Snape Fell, Parlick Pike, Windy Harbour Farm, Old Hive hamlet, Chipping.

If the Access Area over Fair Snape Fell is closed the following alternative route is used from Fiendsdale Head to the lane below Fell Foot farm: Holme House Fell, Holme House Farm, Higher Fair Snape Farm, foot of Parlick Pike. The alternative route is three-quarters of a mile longer than the main route. A map of the alternative route is given in the Appendix.

6. Chipping to Whalley – 13 miles: road to Dairybarn Farm, track and road to Doeford Bridge, Bradley Hall, footpath to top of Longridge Fell, Plantation Farm, Greengore Farm, Dean Brook, Hurst Green, Trough House, River Ribble, Dinckley Hall, Aspinalls Farm, Lower Elker Farm, footpath to Whalley.

Intermediate Distances

The following are suggested breaks for those who do not wish to walk each section in full. For further details of accommodation on the route, please see the 'Additional Information' (page 43).

1. WHALLEY to a) Barley village (7 miles), b) Rimington hamlet, off route, (13 miles).

2. GISBURN to a) Earby village and Youth Hostel, off route, (13 miles), b) Lothersdale (11 miles).

3. SKIPTON to a) Embsay village (2 miles), Cracoe hamlet (8 miles), b) Thorpe hamlet (9 miles), c) Linton village and Youth Hostel (10 miles), d) Threshfield village, off route, (11 miles).

4. MALHAM to a) Settle (6 miles), b) Stainforth Youth Hostel, off route, (9 miles) c) Rathmell village, off route, (10 miles).

5. SLAIDBURN to Dunsop Bridge (via Whitendale valley), off route, (11 miles).

6. CHIPPING to Hurst Green village (7 miles).

An Outline
of the Route

The centre of Whalley – start and finish of The Two Roses Way

SECTION 1:
WHALLEY TO GISBURN

Distance: 15 miles.

Maps: 1:50,000 – Sheet 103; 1:25,000 – SD 63/73, SD 64/74, SD 84/94.

Whalley's name is derived from two Old English words meaning "hillfield" or "field below the hill". St Mary's church, built between 1200 and 1220, has three Celtic crosses in the churchyard, one dating from the 10th century. The cross opposite the south door was damaged when all the crosses were uprooted and thrown into a ditch during the Civil War.

The church has a Roman altar in the north aisle dating back to the 1st century. The original church was founded in 627 and the churchyard is pre-Norman covering three periods: Anglo-Celtic, Anglian and Anglo-Norse.

The Cistercian abbey (established 1330) ruins are close to the church. Much of the abbey masonry was sold off to

The 11thC Celtic cross in St Mary's churchyard, Whalley

local builders in the 1540s and the abbey church was pulled down in the 1660s.

Ruins of the 13thC Cistercian Abbey

On each side of the road leading east out of Whalley there are deposits of gravel and sands left behind by glacial meltwater. Glaciation began almost two million years ago and had periods of retreat and advance, the mos recent glaciation occurring 10,000 years ago. At its highest point, t e Ribblesdale Glacier flowing south-west down the Ribble valley from Yorkshire filled the Calder valley at Whalley and surrounded Pendle Hill and Longridge Fell. The height reached by the ice was such that it overflowed south through gaps in the Wiswell Moor and Pendle ridge, as well as at Weets Hill and Barnoldswick. The Ribblesdale Glacier was joined on the west by ice from the Lake District and boulder deposits from Cumbria have been found in the Cliviger gorge, over 10 miles south-east of Whalley.

Climbing out of the Whalley gorge, the route passes Clerk Hill, one of the historic houses of the Calder valley and the original home of the Whalley family.

On the top of Wiswell (Old English, "marshy stream") Moor is Jeppe Knave's Grave. Jeppe (pronounced "Yep") was a Saxon name and the story goes that he was beheaded for theft in the 11th century. The grave can be easily found using the 1:25,000 map but the story is doubtful and no excavation of the site has been made.

During a period when the Ice Age glaciers were melting , the Sabden valley was occupied by a lake which reached up to the 200 metre (approximately 675 feet) contour. This was a spur of Lake Accrington, which filled the large bowl of land five miles to the south.

The geological map shows that the south-east side of Wiswell Moor is made up of Pendle Grit, while the opposite side of the Sabden valley (Padiham Heights) is capped by Kinderscout Grit, which was formed at a later period. Pendle Grit, like other gritstones, is made up of sediment deposited on the sea floor by major river deltas over 280 million years ago. It rests on beds of Carboniferous Limestone which were deposited at an earlier date on the floor of a clear, relatively shallow sea. Slabs of Pendle Grit can be seen in the small disused quarry at the roadside on the Nick of Pendle.

The woods which can be seen above Sabden (Old English, "valley where fir trees grow") were the home of nightjars in the 19th century, although these birds are no longer found locally on this side of the Ribble valley – the last recorded sighting being in 1945.

A wallcreeper, a very rare South Mediterranean visitor to Britain, was shot in Sabden in 1872 and up until the late 1970s was still on display in Mansfield museum.

Pendle Hill, as named on the Ordnance Survey maps, is nameless in a sense! The first syllable comes from the British for "hill", while the second syllable comes from the Old English for "hill". The Anglo-Saxons added the extra "Hill" on the end, assuming that "Pendle" was the hill's proper name.

Above the 450 metre (1,500 feet) contour on Pendle Hill the surface is covered with post-Ice Age peat which contains in its lower layers the remains of trees such as birch and alder which grew there over 5,000 years ago.

The Pendle ridge, which in geological terms is 20 miles long, is part of the Ribblesdale Fold Belt formed by land movements over 200 million years ago. A process of folding forced up the Pendle ridge and a belt of rock strata extending west-south-west through Skipton and across the Pennine watershed as far east as Harrogate. The first two days of the walk follow the high ground of the Ribblesdale Fold Belt to Skipton.

Official statistics show that Pendle has roughly the same annual rainfall as Malham Tarn, approximately 60 inches per year.

A small population of Red Grouse can be found on Pendle, even though the moorland is not keepered. In 1913, when the top was a grouse moor, the local Press reported that a party of ten guns shot 182 birds on the 12th August. Ravens were recorded on Pendle in the 19th century but have not been seen there in recent times. At least two pairs of merlins used to nest there in the 1930s but the last recorded sighting was in 1952.

The rare dotterel, which winters in North Africa, has been seen on Pendle on two occasions during the 1970s. There are usually a pair or two of dunlin and a small population of golden plover.

Wild boar were hunted on the fell until 1617 and, at an earlier date, wolves and deer were found there also.

Barley (Old English, "clearing where barley is grown") village is in a hollow surrounded by fields of fertile glacial boulder clay and ringed by the higher land of Pendleside Sandstone to the north and Pendle Grit to the south, west and east. The first settlement was established in 1260 when the village was the site of a "vaccary", a Norman cow farm.

Although the top of Rimington Moor is made up of Pendle Grit, once the farm lane near Higher Gills is reached there are limestone strata on either side, deposited up to 50 million years before the gritstone above.

Before reaching Gisburn the route passes through the parishes of Twiston and Rimington, which were Quaker strongholds in the late 17th century. Quakers from the farms of Gazegill, Howgill, and Martin Top (all of which are passed on the route) would meet at Clough Head farm, the home of the Bulcock family. A memorial to the Bulcocks was erected at Clough Head in 1863 and can still be seen there.

Barley village on a Saturday afternoon!

An old corner of Gisburn, once a Yorkshire village in the centre of the Vale of Craven

SECTION 2:
GISBURN TO SKIPTON

Distance: 16 miles.

Maps: 1:50,000 – Sheet 103; 1:25,000 – SD 84/94, Outdoor Leisure Map No. 10, Yorkshire Dales (Southern Area).

The village of Gisburn dates back to at least the 11th century and is the largest settlement between Clitheroe and Skipton. It is now inside the Lancashire border, but at one time the village was regarded as being in the centre of the pasture land known as the Vale of Craven.

The Ribblesdale Arms, in the centre of the village, was built by the Lister family in 1635. Their coat of arms and family motto can be seen on a plaque over the door. The family also established Gisburn Hall and the Park which surrounds it, planting 1,200,000 oaks and an unrecorded number of other trees along the banks of the River Ribble above and below the Park. Cromwell stayed at Gisburn Park in August 1648 when his Parliamentary Army reached Gisburn on the way to Stonyhurst and Preston. The gated entrance to the Park and Hall (which is now a private hospital) can be seen near the Ribblesdale Arms.

Up until the 19th century, Gisburn Park was famous for its herd of wild, white cattle, thought to have been descended from the wild cattle of North Lancashire and the West Riding of Yorkshire. The cattle were pure white except for black tips on their noses, ears and feet. They had no horns and were said to be quite tame. As a result of inbreeding, the flock became delicate and the numbers declined to the point where only bull calves were produced. The last of the cattle were killed off in 1859.

Further back in Gisburn's history, the old ballad of "Guy of Gisburn" tells of a local nobleman's unsuccessful attempt to kill Robin Hood. In medieval times, the colonies of heron which were found along the Ribble near Gisburn Park were regarded as game birds preserved for the nobility to hunt using hawks. Any destruction of the birds by local serfs was severely punished.

In September and October 1974, a pair of white storks, normally found in Scandinavia during the summer months, were observed around Gisburn.

The North Western Railway opened a line passing through Gisburn in the summer of 1849. As the then Lord Ribblesdale of Gisburn Hall was a major shareholder of the company and did not want to see the trains, the line through Gisburn Park was laid in tunnel with "castellated ends, turrets and battlements." These can still be seen a hundred yards down the minor road running north near the New Inn.

At one time, the land and property owned by the Ribblesdale family stretched from Gisburn up to Malham Tarn, but by 1851 the Malham Tarn area had been sold off to Walter Morrison, a friend of John Ruskin the Victorian artist and literary critic. In the 1920s, the last Lord Ribblesdale introduced sika deer into the Park. The original intention was that the stags would be released for hunting and recaptured (those which were not killed anyway!). This did not work out in practice and colonies of sika deer can now be found across a wide area north-west of Gisburn, extending as far as Whitendale in the Forest of Bowland.

In geological terms, the villages of Gisburn and Lothersdale are divided from Skipton by the South Craven Fault. This is part of a multiple fault with three branches (the other two being the Mid and North Craven Faults) each one of them forcing the Great Scar Limestone, typical of the Craven area, higher towards the north. It has been estimated that the total displacement of the rock strata is over 5,000 feet.

Following Coal Pit Lane out of Gisburn, between Lane Side Farm and Weets House the route passes through the succession of rock strata in this area: Pendleside Limestone, Ravensholme Limestone, Pendleside Sandstone and Pendleside Gritstone. The summits of Weets Hill and White Moor (which is a keepered grouse moor) make up a plateau of Pendle gritstone which extends down as far as Green Bank farm before fields of boulder clay are reached once again.

Whitemoor Reservoir was constructed in the late 1850s and is used, together with water from other local reservoirs, to feed the Leeds and Liverpool canal in the valley below. As a large area of upland water it attracts many wildfowl and the following birds have all been observed there: mallard, wigeon, pintail, sanderling, tufted duck, goosander, canada goose, coot and turnstone, together with impressive incoming movements of curlew in the spring.

The route passes the small hamlet of Hey (meaning "place surrounded by a hedge") and continues past Daubers farm where in 1929 a 17th century written charm (used to ward off evil spirits) was discovered.

The Leeds and Liverpool canal is crossed at Daubers Bridge. Locally, work on the canal began in 1790, although the complete canal had been started in the 1770s and took almost twenty years to finish.

The canal is 127 miles long and reaches its highest point above sea-level (487 feet) near to where the route crosses it. Half a mile south of Daubers Bridge the canal passes through the Foulridge Tunnel which is 1,640 yards long and took five years to complete, becoming the single most expensive item of the whole canal project. Because of soft soil, over half of the tunnel could not be tunnelled in the traditional way but had to be dug out as a channel and then roofed over afterwards.

The lives of the navvies who constructed the Tunnel were held so cheap that some of those who were killed during the work were simply buried along the canal banks.

The section of the canal which includes the Foulridge Tunnel was completed in 1796. As the Tunnel has no towpath, from 1796 up until the 1880s barges were "legged" through by men pushing against the roof with their feet. The leggers could push a loaded boat through in an hour, or half an hour if the boat was empty.

For those who have time to stop for a drink in the Hole in the Wall pub (said to be named after the Tunnel entrance) just down the road in Foulridge village, there is a photograph on the wall of Buttercup the cow which, in 1912, fell into the canal at the far end and swam right through. As the Tunnel is almost a mile long, it is understandable that she had to be hauled out and treated with alcohol at the Foulridge end. In the early

19th century several other local pubs (now defunct) took their names from associations with the canal, including the "Grinning Rat" and the "Slip Inn".

The Leeds and Liverpool canal as a whole was a commercially successful enterprise for over 130 years, with profits being paid to shareholders from 1786 to 1919.

The area around Daubers Bridge marks a watershed between Lancashire and Yorkshire. The small stream crossed by a footbridge beyond the canal flows north into Earby Beck and then on into the River Aire at Carleton, near Skipton. Streams flowing south from Foulridge drain into Colne Water and Pendle Water and eventually into the Lancashire River Calder.

Just before reaching the A56 near Foulridge, the path of the old Colne-Skipton railway line is crossed. The line operated until 1970 but the station at Foulridge was closed in 1959.

Foulridge (pronounced "Foalridge") takes its name from the combination of the Anglo-Saxon "fola" (foal) and "hyreg" (ridge) and is thought to have been established as a settlement by Angles in the 7th century. The route follows the ridge where the settlers are supposed to have grazed their foals. The village of Earby (three miles away) was first colonised by Danes in the early 10th century. Earlier still, the Celtic walling at the foot of Noyna Hill indicates that the area was settled by Brigantes during the Iron Age.

In the valley at Foulridge there are deposits of glacial sand and gravel left by overflow ice from the main glacier occupying the Ribble Valley. The route follows the gritstone fells out of Foulridge, with Warley Wise Grit from the A56 to Copy House and Pendle Grit from Hawshaw to Ramshaw and down to the Aire valley.

On Noyna Hill the route passes above Oxenards farm, which probably takes its name from the pasturing of oxen by early settlers.

Teddy Carr's Drive (the farm lane running past Oxenards) is named after Edward Carr of Langroyd Hall who bought all the farms on the road in the 19th century so that he would have a private route up to his shooting lodge on the side of Kelbrook Moor.

The recently renovated lodge and Teddy Carr's Moor are now owned by a shooting syndicate.

Half a mile south of Copy House farm there is a building with the unusual name of Jerusalem which was at one time a smallpox isolation hospital and later a Youth Hostel. On Kelbrook Moor, near the Lancashire-Yorkshire border, there is a "Dissenters' Well", indicating that this was a meeting place for those who dissented from the established church at a time when legislation prevented such religious meetings within five miles of a Parish Church.

The Pinfold

Many visitors to Lothersdale village miss the site of the "Pinfold", opposite the Hare and Hounds, where, up until 1905, stray animals were impounded.

Half a mile east along the road from the village is Stonegappe house where Charlotte Brontë was a governess and which she portrays as "Gateshead" in Jane Eyre. In the early 20th century this was the home of Clare Delius, the sister of Frederick Delius the composer. While Delius was staying at Stonegappe he used to walk from there to Haworth and, because of the Brontë associations of the house and the surrounding area, he once thought of setting Wuthering Heights to music.

The descent off Ramshaw moor marks the end of the central ridge of the Pennines which can be regarded as beginning at Standedge and continuing north as a series of high plateaux.

The valley of the Aire was used by the Romans for the road they constructed linking Ribchester, Ilkley and York. Three thousand years before, Bronze Age traders travelling from Ireland to Scandinavia also used this gap through the Pennines.

The youthful River Aire and the Aire Gap at Carleton Bridge

Skipton, like Earby, was a 10th century Danish colony. Several hundred years prior to this, in the 2nd and 4th centuries, the "wild hill men" of Skipton took part in uprisings against the occupying Romans.

They destroyed forts and villas and forced the Romans to take protection from the limestone caves in the Craven uplands to the west. The exhibits in the Craven Museum in the Town Hall on High Street include Brigantian swords from 50 AD as well as items which illustrate other aspects of the history, geology, and archaeology of the area.

Skipton Castle, which probably dates from about 1090, is considered to be one of the best preserved examples of a medieval castle in Britain. The route passes the castle entrance and the motto "Desormais", which can be seen above the gateway, means "Henceforward". This was the motto of the Earls of Cumberland and the tomb of George, the third Earl of Cumberland, can be found in the parish church next to the castle. As well as Skipton Castle, the Cumberlands also owned Appleby Castle and Brougham Castle in Westmorland.

The Leeds and Liverpool canal in Skipton

Skipton Castle was one of the subjects sketched by Joseph Turner, the artist, in July 1816 on a tour which included Gordale Scar, Browsholme Hall and the Trough of Bowland. Just to prove that summers in the early 19th century were not necessarily any better than today, he described the sketching trip as an "insufferably wet expedition".

The entrance to Skipton Castle. "DESORMAIS" is the motto of the Earls of Cumberland

SECTION 3:
SKIPTON TO MALHAM

Distance: 18 miles. **Maps:** 1:50,000 – Sheet 98; 1:25,000 – Outdoor Leisure Map No. 10, Yorkshire Dales (Southern Area)

IMPORTANT NOTE: Before leaving Skipton a decision must be made whether to use the Embsay Moor Access Area *en route* to Linton or to take the alternative route, using public footpaths, shown in the Appendix. Both routes are equal in distance. At certain times of the year the Embsay Moor Access Area is closed. Before setting off to use the Access Area check that the route is open by telephoning the Grassington National Park Information Centre, Colvend, Grassington, Skipton, North Yorkshire (Tel. 0756 752774). The route as described in the text assumes that the Access Area is open. The alternative route shown in the Appendix rejoins the main route at Linton village.

The route leaves Skipton, passing the 11th century parish church of Holy Trinity (substantially rebuilt in the 14th and 16th centuries) and the Norman castle, before following a minor road to Embsay. A steam railway operates from here at weekends and Bank Holidays. The line, built by the Midland railway in 1888, is now owned by the Yorkshire Dales Railway Trust and operates on a two mile stretch from Embsay to Holywell.

Beyond the village is the Embsay Moor Access Area and the walk continues along the western boundary of the moor, following a path over Crookrise Crag, Rylstone Fell and Cracoe Fell at approximately the 400 metre (1,300 feet) contour. The area is covered with gritstone outcrops.

Rylstone Cross, overlooking the village of the same name, was originally a large stone in the form of a man. A wooden cross was erected on top of the stone pillar to commemorate the "Peace of Paris" in 1885. It has been replaced several times, the last occasion being in 1947.

Rylstone Cross

One of Wordsworth's later poems, The White Doe of Rylstone, contains the following lines,

> *Nor lacked she Reason's firmest power;*
> *But with the White Doe at her side*
> *Up she would climb to Norton Tower,*
> *And thence look round her far and wide...*

The remains of Norton Tower are half a mile south-east of Rylstone Cross and 400 feet below, so Wordsworth's heroine, Emily, probably did not have such a wide-ranging viewpoint.

In Rylstone village is a building known as "Fox House Barn", now a private house. It was named after George Fox and built in 1657 as a Quaker Meeting House.

A mile further up the valley is the village of Cracoe where there are a number of 17th century "longhouses". The stone for these was quarried locally from the surrounding fells. On the top of Cracoe Fell stands an obelisk to commemorate those killed in the First World War. The cairn was blown down several times before a local craftsman was engaged to complete the structure. In 1923 he took a tent up to the site and stayed on the fell until the monument had been built.

Cracoe War Memorial

The route descends through Rolling Gate Crags and Raven Nest Crags to the hamlet of Thorpe, a cluster of cottages, guest house and farm. It is easy to see why Thorpe was used as a refuge for women and children during the Scots border raids in the Middle Ages. It gained the reputation of being the place the Scots could never find.

Turning north-west, we approach the picturesque village of Linton where the houses, cottages and farms surround a wide, rectangular green which slopes gently down to the beck. The beck is crossed by three bridges and a shallow ford. The pack-horse bridge (14th century) was repaired by Dame Elizabeth Redmayne in the 17th century. It is said that local farmers refused to contribute to the repairs so she added a narrow parapet to prevent carts crossing the bridge.

The village green and bridge at Linton

The spinning of flax, which grew in abundance in the area, was a major occupation in the village up to the 18th century. There are still examples in the village of the stone "retting" troughs in which the flax was rotted. It is probable that Linton derives its name from flax (Lin).

At the southern end of the village stands an imposing building, Fountaine Hospital. Richard Fountaine, who was born in the village and went on to become an Alderman of the City of London, bequeathed money in 1721 to provide an almshouse for "six poor men and women". His name is also given to the Inn which overlooks the green.

The route continues towards Threshfield (with views of the fine Dales village of Grassington across the valley of the River Wharfe) before following a green lane over Threshfield Moor and dropping down to the Bordley valley. From there we climb again to Weets Top before descending via Hawthorns Lane to Gordale Scar and Malham dale. In addition to being a very attractive tourist destination with its extensive footpath system and miles of limestone walls, the whole area around Malham village is designated as a Site of Special Scientific Interest.

Gordale Scar (half a mile off the route) is hidden from view until you are almost upon it. The Scar was once a vast underground cavern before the roof was eroded away. The cascading waterfall is a spectacular sight, particularly after heavy rain. The Scar and the gorge above owe their origins to erosion by Ice Age glacier meltwater.

Gordale Scar

Malham village, with its hump-backed bridge, village green and stream, consists of a cluster of houses, cottages, a smithy, cafes, inns, and a Youth Hostel. Many of the buildings were erected in the 17th and 18th centuries with walls of limestone and roofs of gritstone or slate. A feature of the area is the abundance of well maintained limestone dry-stone walls, sometimes reaching far up the crag faces. Some of the walls date back to the period when Fountains Abbey and Bolton Priory grazed sheep on the fells.

Malham stands at the head of Airedale and was established as a farming community in the 7th and 8th centuries. The Beck which flows through the middle of the village provided the monastic boundary between the domains of Fountains Abbey to the west and Bolton Priory to the east. "Monk Bridge", the main bridge across the Beck, may have been a crossing place which was jointly constructed by the two institutions.

The whole of the route from Skipton to Malham passes through an area rich in mineral sources. In a previous era, iron ore and lead were mined. Quarrying for limestone is still carried out, as also is quarrying for magnesium silicate which is processed into talc.

The impressive escarpment running east to west and including the 240 feet high Malham Cove and Gordale Scar, follows the line of the North Craven Fault. At one time the stream flowing out of Malham Tarn followed the dry valley above the Cove and poured over the edge in a waterfall greater than Niagara Falls. On the top of the Cove there is a limestone pavement created when the Ice Age was receding. The escarpment marks the divide between Great Scar Limestone to the north and Bowland shale and reef limestone to the south.

The area is also rich in wildlife, with flowers such as dog's mercury, ramsons, Pennine whitebeam and mountain pansies. On the moorland heights, birds such as kestrels, buzzards, red grouse and twite can be seen, with kingfishers, dippers, redshanks, curlew and snipe on the lower land.

SECTION 4:
MALHAM TO SLAIDBURN

Distance: 19 miles.

Maps: 1:50,000 – Sheets 98, 103; 1:25,000 – Outdoor Leisure Map No. 10, Yorkshire Dales (Southern Area), SD 66/76, SD 65/75.

The way forward takes you a short walk northwards along Cove Road for approximately 250 yards where, opposite Moon Bridge, we turn left up an enclosed bridlepath. Moon Bridge is a simple stone footbridge crossing Malham Beck and was named after the last Augustinian Prior of Bolton Abbey.

The path proceeds under two limestone outcrops, Hoober Edge and Hanber Side which form part of Pikedaw Hill. In this vicinity are many derelict mine shafts and workings. Note too the differing type of dry stone-walling as you make the steady ascent: to the left is Millstone Grit, to the right limestone. Half a mile further you join the ancient bridleway running between Malham and Settle. At Nappa Gate there is a junction of tracks. For those who have time, Nappa Cross (originally a wayside cross) has been preserved in the wall approximately 200 yards northwards along the Langscar track. Stop here a short while to take in the breath-taking landscape – Malham dale, the Cove and Tarn, Fountains Fell, Penyghent and part of Ribblesdale.

The bridleway continues westward picking up the emerging Stockdale Beck which drops to the farm of that name. Stockdale Farm lies along the Craven Fault and you can observe the changing countryside: north of the beck is the range of limestone crags and outcrops, whilst to the south the moorland is characteristic of Millstone Grit. The route follows a path which skirts Attermire Scar and Warrendale Knotts.

The name Attermire originates from the marshy ground in the shallow valley, which was once a tarn formerly known as Otters Mire. The area has numerous caves, the most notable being Attermire, Victoria and

Jubilee, all within a short distance of the route. Victoria Cave was named because its hidden entrance was discovered on Queen Victoria's Coronation Day in 1838. Part of the floor of the cave has a fossilised clay surface with the marks of ancient water ripples. In several of the caves, prehistoric relics of mammoth, rhinoceros, bison and long-tusked elephant have been found and some are now displayed in the museum on Chapel Street in Settle.

Attermire Scar and Warrendale Knotts

Continue along the path, which drops steeply giving a panoramic view across Settle and Ribblesdale, with the green copper dome of Giggleswick School chapel in the distance. The original school was established in 1512 but the chapel and dome was a gift from Walter Morrison of Malham Tarn House to celebrate Queen Victoria's Diamond Jubilee.

Settle, capital of north Ribblesdale is a thriving community drawing many tourists and travellers who wander the many narrow streets and alleyways in this historic town. The River Ribble, the Settle to Carlisle

Railway and the busy A65 Leeds to Kendal trunk road all flow through the town. The Market Place is the hub, it has a bustling outdoor market each Tuesday.

The Square in Settle

Around the open square is the fine Elizabethan-style Town Hall (built in 1832) and the 17th century Shambles, with its living quarters opening onto a gallery above a filled in arcade. A cafe in the Market Place was once an inn called the Naked Man and has a stone effigy with the date in a strategic position.

As a cafe it provides excellent nourishment and hospitality for the weary traveller. In the Church near the railway viaduct is a marble plaque commemorating the many workmen who lost their lives in the district when the railway was built between 1869 and 1876.

The town's history goes back beyond the Market which was granted a charter in 1248. Emerging from prehistory, north of the town is the Celtic Wall. Even today it stands in good condition at 65 feet long and 5 feet thick, although no one is sure just what its purpose was. Castlebergh is another landmark which over looks the town. Its fortress-like crag is topped by a flagpole erected to commemorate Queen Victoria's accession to the throne in 1837. The crag is Settle's civic symbol and was even engraved on locally produced banknotes during the last century. Notable son's of Settle included Benjamin Waugh, founder of the National Society for the Prevention of Cruelty to Children. Dr George Birkbeck was another, he founded the mechanics institutes and is also remembered in the name of Birkbeck College, London.

The route follows the River Ribble out of Settle and coincides with the Ribble Way for the two miles to Hollin Hall. On the opposite side of the river, near Penny Bridge, can be seen a line of beech trees, many of them over 100 years old, which serve as the boundary to Anley House.

The route leaves North Yorkshire and returns to Lancashire by passing unceremoniously through a gap in the millstone grit dry-stone wall near Hanover Gill.

The Ribble at Settle – at 500 feet above sea-level, still an upland river

Stocks Reservoir, surrounded by the conifers of Gisburn Forest, is the only reservoir in the Forest of Bowland. On the road side, near to the causeway across the reservoir, stands the little chapel of St James, Dalehead.

The chapel of St James, Dalehead; be sure to sign the visitors' book to show you have passed this quiet place

It was moved to this site from half a mile away when the reservoir was built in the 1920s. The head of the Hodder valley was submerged behind a 440 yard dam and the hamlet of Stocks-in-Bowland, together with four farms, disappeared beneath the reservoir.

Slaidburn nestles in a hollow beside the River Hodder and up until 1974 it was within the Yorkshire boundary. It was a settlement of some importance in medieval times, being the administrative centre of the Royal Forest of Bowland. The court for the area was held upstairs in the building which is now the "Hark to Bounty" and the old court-room is still preserved. The court rolls also record the building of a court in 1577 on the site where the primary school now stands. Now predominantly a farming community with a steady influx of visitors, it also used to have a thriving woollen industry and a corn mill. The village boasted a Grammar School built in 1712, which is now the local primary school. The Church of St Andrews founded in the 11th century stands sentinel over the southern approach to the village and once used to ring the local curfew. It retains its Jacobean chancel screen and three-decker pulpit.

The drinking fountain in Slaidburn

SECTION 5:
SLAIDBURN TO CHIPPING

Distance: 18 miles.

Maps: 1:50,000 – Sheets 102, 103; 1:25,000 – SD 65/75, SD 44/54, SD 64/74

IMPORTANT NOTE: Part of the route follows the Fair Snape Fell Access Area. At certain times of the year the Access Area may be closed. If the Access Area is closed, the alternative route shown in the Appendix should be used from Fiendsdale Head to the lane below Fell Foot farm. The alternative route is three-quarters of a mile longer than the main route.

It is believed that the name "Slaidburn" comes from the word "slaid", a slab of stone which was said to mark the site of a great battle in the area.

The sign at the "Hark to Bounty Inn" shows a clergyman listening to a dog baying at the full moon. There are various explanations of how the inn got its name. One such is that Bounty was a leading foxhound (a "bosshound") belonging to the Rev. Wigglesworth, the 19th century rector and squire of the parish. He would leave the dog outside the inn and when it barked would say to his companions, "Hark to Bounty".

The Brennand valley cuts deep into the heart of the Forest of Bowland. This area was farmed by the Parker family of Browsholme Hall whose name arose from their duty as keepers of the Forest of Bowland. Bowland's status as royal hunting territory lasted right up until the 16th century.

It is likely that the highest fells of the Forest of Bowland were not covered by ice during the last Ice Age, although there are many examples of the effects of glacial action on the upland cols, such as the passes at the Trough of Bowland, Salter Fell and Cross of Greet. Much of the area was surrounded by major glaciers flowing from the Lake District and Lonsdale.

The Trough of Bowland and Whins Brow

The underlying strata is gritstone with a surface covering of blanket peat. This is a high upland area, covering 803 square kilometres (310 square miles), with hills rising to over 1,800 feet, drained by the River Ribble to the south and the River Lune to the north.

The Forest of Bowland was designated as an Area of Outstanding Natural Beauty in 1964 but, despite this, it still remains relatively little visited compared with the adjoining Craven Dales.

There is very little free access to the Bowland fells, apart from a major public bridleway running roughly north-east to south-west (used by the route) and the Clougha, Fair Snape, Wolf Fell and Saddle Fell Access Agreement areas created in 1973. These give access to limited areas in the north-west and south west of Bowland, leaving the majority of the fells open only to their private owners.

Much of the upland is managed for grouse shooting and sheep grazing. The pass at the top of the Trough of Bowland road is on the dividing line between the fells to the north-west which are "owned" by the Duke of Westminster and the south-western fells "owned" by North West Water. As far as access is concerned, little seems to have changed since medieval times when large parts of the area were Royal Hunting Forests restricted to the nobility.

Langden valley water intake and Sykes Nab, guarding the approach to Fiendsdale

The water authority intake at the mouth of the Langden valley was originally constructed to provide water for Preston, with the water being treated and stored at Longridge. The valley and the surrounding fells are owned by North West Water, although the grandly named "Langden Castle" was built as a shooting hut.

The Langden valley provides an interesting study of an upland water course and shows that change is constantly taking place. Langden Brook, in common with most Bowland streams, carries peat debris, sand eroded from the river bed and glacial outwash. Studies have classified the course of the Brook as a "braided channel" and this feature can be seen quite clearly in the upper reaches.

The stream divides into subsidiary channels, like braids, which are not permanent but are subject to shoal formation and channel widening, leading to the creation of new channels and the abandonment of the old course. These processes can occur rapidly during flooding or over longer periods – as one study of the valley showed, a channel created by flooding in 1975 had been abandoned by 1983. The gullies which can be seen cutting into the sides of the Langden valley run out into alluvial fans which contain ancient tree remains. This indicates that the process which created the gullies began while the valley was still wooded and very much different in appearance than it is today.

This area is included within the Nature Conservancy Council's "Bowland Fells Site of Special Scientific Interest" as it contains the largest expanse of heather moorland in Lancashire, provides a variety of upland habitats, and is the breeding ground for birds of prey such as the hen harrier, merlin and peregrine falcon.

Three or four thousand years ago, Bronze Age men hunted on Parlick Pike and established a stockaded village of beehive huts among the swamps of Bleasdale.

"Chipping" in Old English means market ("cheapings"). In the 17th century, the village provided the main market for this area of Lancashire. John Brabin, a local dyer and dealer in cloth who died in 1683 left funds, for the poor and for the building of the local village school and almshouses which are still standing. He built and lived in the house which is now the post office. The Brabin trustees were still administering the granting of occupation in the almshouses in the early 1980s.

St Bartholomew's church tower was built in about 1450, although the main body of the church was rebuilt in 1506 and restored in 1873. One of Chipping's vicars, John Milner, was a close friend of John Wesley and accompanied him on a preaching tour through northern England and Scotland. Wesley preached in Chipping in 1752 but when he returned the following year he was shouted down by a group of parishioners.

SECTION 6:
CHIPPING TO WHALLEY

Distance: 13 miles.

Maps: 1:50,000 – Sheet 103; 1:25,000 – SD 64/74, SD 63/73

Chipping has been well-covered in books of walks and tourist literature, and quite rightly so. It is a lovely little village reflecting so many aspects of the hidden beauty of this area and of the two counties of Lancashire and Yorkshire. Visiting walkers, burdened perhaps with images drawn from limited classroom economic history and contemporary soaps, will by now have merged image with reality.

Rural craft industry was, of course, here before the industrial revolution. Rush-seated chairs and stools made by hand have been produced in Chipping over several centuries (dating back to the cottage industry) and they are still in production.

H.J.Berry, Chairmakers, was founded in 1840 by John Berry, who also doubled as the landlord of the local Sun Inn. The firm is now in its fifth generation of family ownership, employs about 120 people, and specialises in chairs, tables and stools – some 600 per day on full production. Over 50% of the timber used ends up as waste which is burnt to heat the drying kilns and tunnels, the polishing rooms and the main factory.

The Kirk Mill Waterwheel first drove machinery in the then cotton mill an estimated 200 years ago – it was turned to chairmaking use in the 1880s. 30 feet in diameter and 6 feet wide, it is one of the largest waterwheels in the country, although the Saunders Rake Works wheel in Chipping was 45 feet in diameter. In 1923 the waterwheel was providing electricity for the works and the village – it came to a full stop in 1943.

Leaving by the Clitheroe road, the walk takes us along the valley bottom towards the last fell on this circular route. The name of the first farm reached, Dairy Barn, reflects the fact that Lancashire farming is more "milk" than arable. Around here, in the first half of this century, the dairy shorthorn was the main breed. Today, nationally, the black and white Friesian has taken over. It gives much more milk and is a popular beef cross with a Hereford or one of the increasing number of imported continental breeds. The calf of the Hereford cross is permanently recognisable by the all-white face of the father. The more mature amongst us will easily remember the Hereford as the regular backdrop herd in the old Westerns.

Longridge Fell, the last climb on The Two Roses Way

Further down the valley, Cherry Tree Farm runs a pedigree herd of Ayrshires. Walkers may have been puzzled from time to time by the sight of the forlorn figure of a single white and red Ayrshire grazing amongst a large dairy herd of black and whites. The reason is a simple one. The "solid-not-fat" content of the Ayrshire milk is included in with the thinner milk of the Friesian to safeguard the requirement for the monthly milk cheque.

The other major change, nationally and locally, is the move away from hay to silage as the main grown stock feed. Given our variable summer climate, this makes things more manageable for the farmer. But it has brought with it greater problems of pollution as seepage of harmful effluent from silage bays finds its way into rivers and the water system. The carefree application of nitrates on the land has also contributed to water pollution.

The 28-stalled herringbone milking parlour at Bradley Hall (1851) is an example of the many improvements in dairy farming during the post-war years. The Hall leads us on to Longridge Fell, the first of the day and the last of the Two Roses Way.

In the fields on the way up the Fell you may come across some Jacob's sheep – black and white like the Friesians but a rare breed category, now making a come-back. "As old as the Book of Genesis", it is claimed. They are good mothers and may be polled or carry two, four or six horns. They provide a quality fleece with natural colours which does not need bleaching or dying.

Longridge Fell provides one of the finest views out of the many of the past days. Looking north across the valley there is the long southern escarpment of the Forest of Bowland. From the left, Parlick Pike rises to Fair Snape Fell – the route down to Chipping. Continuing left, there are the Wolf, Saddle, Burnslack, Fair Oak and Totteridge Fells. Next, there is the gap in the escarpment where the beautiful Hodder valley runs down to meet the River Loud. To the right of the Hodder valley are the smaller Birkett and Hodder Bank Fells. Following the line of the Hodder valley northwards leads to the eastern escarpment of Bowland, with Burn Fell and Beatrix Fell in view. Further right is Easington Fell, followed by Grindleton Fell, Waddington Fell and Browsholme Moor.

Up there as well is the "Centre of the British Isles" – in 1991 the Ordnance Survey officially declared it so. The first location was a site at Cromwell's Bridge, Chaigley. It was then found that the calculations failed to include the islands around Britain and the centre was finally pinpointed ten miles north at a point near Whitendale Rocks. British Telecom sited their 100,000 payphone at Dunsop Bridge, the nearest village to the centre of Britain.

Before we turn away, the Loud valley below provides a chessboard picture of enclosed fields – refreshingly durable compared with the monotonous CAP-encouraged arable prairies of East Anglia and elsewhere.

The Ribble valley is once again before us, with Pendle to the left and the West Pennine Moors also on the horizon. Our map takes us steadily down good tracks past Lennox Farm and Dean Brook, with the towers of Stonyhurst College indicating Hurst Green close at hand. Further examples of stonewall craftsmanship present themselves, matching those of the Yorkshire Dales. Dry stone walling demands a lot of skills: an eye and feel for shape, weight, size and bridging potential, and a constant judicious selection from the starting mound of stones. The technique involves starting from a wide base with "footing" stones and creating an outer layer of large stones with an inner rubble filling called "hearting". Stability is provided by "throughs", stones which pass through the centre of the wall and join the outer layers. The top of the wall usually has sloping "cam" stones. An Enclosure Act specification for basic wall dimensions and construction laid down a height of four feet six inches and two layers of throughs.

Stonyhurst College is a centuries old Catholic public school of national standing, well worth a minor diversion simply to enjoy the fine view on the approach road to the main College. It started out in the 16th century in France before the hostility of the Bourbons and the momentum of the French Revolution forced a retreat to the Ribble Valley in 1794. Considered to be representative of the respected Jesuit intellectual arm of the Church, the College has at present about 400 boys and a recent small recruitment of A level girls, taken from both home and overseas. As you would expect, it has extensive playing fields and, in particular, its rugby teams sustain a traditionally high standard of play on the college circuit.

One certainty of life is that one has to sleep somewhere. Oliver Cromwell did so here, in 1648, before dealing with the locals at the Battle of Preston. For some unexplained reason he settled down in full armour on a table in the old Refectory. In those days, friends easily becoming foes, it was perhaps understandable that one eye was never closed. The future historian will also record that the College library was where the count took place for the Ribble Valley by-election, with a result that finally convinced the Conservative Government to do away with the Poll Tax.

Hurst Green is another Lancashire village popular with both walker and tourist and provides the usual amenities for those passing through. The Shireburn Arms takes its name from a family which was prominent in the history of the locality.

The Eagle and Child and the old bottom bar hold fond memories for this walker, with boots outside enjoying a pint and the comradeship of the close friend this book remembers.

Hurst Green

At Dinckley Bridge, just below the village, we meet up again with the waymark and logo of the Ribble Way. Like The Two Roses Way, it bridges the rival counties. It differs in that its starting point is the sea and that, seventy miles later, it finishes at the claimed source of the River Ribble. The path was opened by Mike Harding, President of the Ramblers' Association (RA), in June 1985, although the idea for the walk went back as far as 1967 when a group of RA members from Fylde and Preston, prompted perhaps by the success of the Pennine Way, convened a meeting which was the basis of the original steering committee.

Dinckley suspension bridge over the mature River Ribble; at 100 feet above sea-level, the lowest point on the route

There may be some debate about the true source of the Ribble but there is no doubt about the application and stamina of these RA members – walkers are permanently in debt to the RA for the work it does. The enthusiasts met with the usual and expected "dugout" response from individual and institutional entrenched self-interest. The route and line was altered a number of times over the years. Determination, with the financial support of the Countryside Commission and the extensive practical backup of the County Council, led to the eventual opening ceremony at Edisford Bridge in the Ribble Valley.

Brockhall Hospital comes into view as we come up from the Ribble and follow the route to the Black Bull and Old Langho. In 1916 it served as a place of care for the inebriate. By the 1930s it was a hospital and home for the mentally ill and the mentally handicapped. It developed to become the largest of its type in the country and at one time had over 2,000 residents, 1,500 staff, and covered some 350 acres.

It became a little village in its own right with, its own farm and other facilities, self-contained in many respects, with residents arriving and not knowing any other home for the rest of their lives.

The early part of this century saw a number of institutions grouped in the Ribble Valley or nearby. Within a radius of three or four miles there was Ribchester Workhouse, Blackburn Orphanage at Wilpshire, the Female Inebriate Asylum at Old Langho (which later became Brockhall Hospital for Mental Defectives) and Calderstones Hospital at Whalley.

Part of the explanation for this concentration is said to be the fact that the sites belonged to a small number of very large estates whose owners either needed or wanted to sell off land. Other factors certainly included the relatively sparse local population and the open countryside.

Brockhall closed in 1992 and nearly all the others have gone or are down for closure in the future. Modern drugs have had moderating effects on mental and social disabilities, with continued success in the research field. Much will depend on future political priorities and financial provision as the civilised move towards care in the community continues.

The church and Black Bull at Old Langho leave us with a short way to go to complete the day and the walk.

Afterword

The final day's commentary is inseparable from continuous thoughts of shared walks and close friendship over twenty years with Ken Slater, who was one of the original authors of this book. He was at home with his boots on and he loved the tops – the magnificent Roof of Wales walk, which he did on his own, gave him particular satisfaction from among the many long-distance paths he completed. Today's line and its nice mix always gave him quiet pleasure. But there was, above all, always another mountain to challenge and enjoy. His life was a commitment to, and concern for, the service of others. He tackled this daily challenge as he did his mountains.

ADDITIONAL
INFORMATION

Accommodation

1. WHALLEY TO GISBURN (Ribble Valley district)

"The Ribble Valley Guide", available free from Clitheroe Tourist Information Centre, Council Offices, Church Walk, Clitheroe, Lancashire. Telephone (0200) 25566.

"Lancashire Farmhouse Accommodation", available free from Public Relations Section, Lancashire County Council, County Hall, Preston, Lancashire. Telephone (0772) 54868.

2. GISBURN TO SKIPTON (Pendle and Craven districts)

Pendle district – Gisburn to Copy House Farm

"Lancashire Farmhouse Accommodation", available free from Public Relations Section, Lancashire County Council, details above.

"Pendle Discovery Guide – where to stay, where to eat, what to see and do", available free from Nelson Tourist Information Centre, 20 Scotland Road, Nelson, Lancashire. Telephone (0282) 692890.

Earby Youth Hostel, Glen Cottage, Birch Hall Lane, Earby, Colne, Lancashire. Telephone (0282) 842349.

Craven district – Copy House Farm to Skipton

"Yorkshire Dales Accommodation Guide", available free from Skipton Tourist Information Centre, 8 Victoria Square, Skipton, North Yorkshire. Telephone (0756) 792809. Also available from Grassington National Park Information Centre, Colvend, Hebden Road, Grassington, Skipton, North Yorkshire. Telephone (0756) 752774.

"Where to stay in Skipton and District", available free from Skipton Tourist Information Centre (details as above).

3. SKIPTON TO MALHAM (Craven district)

"Yorkshire Dales Accommodation Guide" (details as above).

"Where to stay in Skipton and District" (details as above).

Linton Youth Hostel, The Old Rectory, Linton in Craven, Skipton, North Yorkshire. Telephone (0756) 752400.

Malham Youth Hostel, John Dower Memorial Hostel, Malham, Skipton, North Yorkshire. Telephone (07293) 321.

4. MALHAM TO SLAIDBURN (Craven and Ribble Valley districts)

Craven district – Malham to Gisburn Forest

"Yorkshire Dales Accommodation Guide" (details as above).

"Where to stay in Skipton and District" (details as above).

Stainforth Youth Hostel, "Taitlands", Stainforth, Settle, North Yorkshire. Telephone (07292) 3577.

Ribble Valley district – Gisburn Forest to Slaidburn

"The Ribble Valley Guide" (details as above).

Slaidburn Youth Hostel, King's House, Slaidburn, Clitheroe, Lancashire. Telephone (02006) 656.

5. SLAIDBURN TO CHIPPING (Ribble Valley district)

"The Ribble Valley Guide" (details as above).

"Lancashire Farmhouse Accommodation" (details as above).

Youth Hostels Association Camping Barns, The Bowland Barns, Booking Office, 16 Shawbridge Street, Clitheroe, Lancashire. Telephone (0200) 28366.

6. CHIPPING TO WHALLEY (Ribble Valley district)

See Section 5 above.

Useful Addresses

Tourist Information Centres

RIBBLE VALLEY DISTRICT:
Clitheroe Tourist Information Centre, Council Offices, Church Walk, Clitheroe, Lancashire. Telephone (0200) 25566.

PENDLE DISTRICT:
Nelson Tourist Information Centre, 20 Scotland Road, Nelson, Lancashire. Telephone (0282) 692890.

Barnoldswick Information Centre, The Old Library, Fernlea Avenue, Barnoldswick, Colne, Lancashire. Telephone (0282) 817046

Barley Picnic Site (restricted opening). Telephone (0282) 601893.

CRAVEN DISTRICT:
Skipton Tourist Information Centre, 8 Victoria Square, Skipton, North Yorkshire. Telephone (0756) 792809.

Grassington National Park Information Centre, Colvend, Hebden Road, Grassington, Skipton, North Yorkshire. Telephone (0756) 752774.

Malham National Park Information Centre (summer opening only), Telephone (0729) 830363.

Settle Tourist Information Centre, Town Hall, Cheapside, Settle, North Yorkshire. Telephone (0729) 825192.

NATIONAL ORGANISATIONS:
Youth Hostels Association, Trevelyan House, 8 St Stephen's Hill, St Albans, Hertfordshire. AL1 2DY. Telephone (0727) 55215.

Ramblers' Association, 1/5 Wandsworth Road, London. SW8 2XX. Telephone (071) 582 6878. The Ramblers' Association produces an accommodation guide for members.

Public Transport

Details of local public transport can be obtained by telephone from the Tourist Information Centres listed above.

Sketch Maps

MAP KEY

Indicates the alignment of each page in respect to grid north. The route is read from the bottom of each page upwards. North is not necessarily at the top of the page.

MAP SCALE: 5" = 1 mile

Line of route ‑‑‑‑‑‑‑‑‑ (not necessarily a footpath on ground)
Road, lane or track enclosed by walls ⌇⌇⌇⌇⌇⌇
Unfenced road, lane or track ‑ ‑ ‑ ‑ ‑
Wall ∞∞∞∞∞∞∞∞∞∞
Broken wall ∞ ∞∞ ∘ ∘   Contours ·······500········
Fence ++++++++++   (these are shown at
Hedge ⅏⅏⅏⅏⅏⅏⅏   100' intervals except
Building ■   where smaller intervals
Ruin □   aid clarity)
Bridge ⌤
Rock outcrop 🪨   Railway line ⊢+⊢+⊢
Boulders ∴∴⋰   Canal ═══
Embankment ▾▾▾▾▾   Rushes ⋎⋏⋎⋏
Triangulation pillar ▲   P.H. : Public house
Decidvous trees ❀❀❀❀   P.O. : Post office
Coniferous trees ♠♠♠♠   F.P. : Footpath
Stream ∼∼∼∼   F.B. : Footbridge
River ≋≋≋   (arrows indicating flow)
Reservoir △▨▨△   Y.H. : Youth Hostel
Pond ♡   Height in feet: e.g., 1,230'
Cairn ✳
Feature identified by a note on map: ✕ (e.g., telephone box)
Miles from start ⌁⌁⌁
(26)

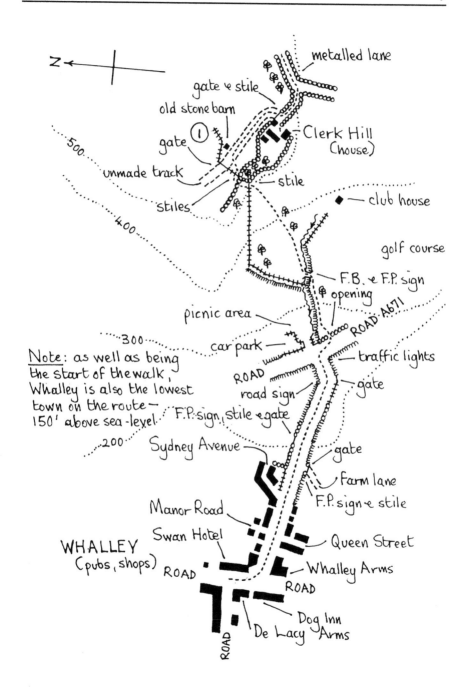

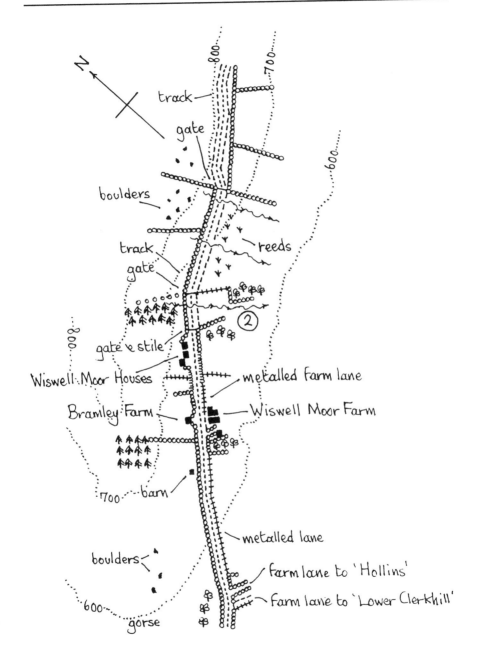

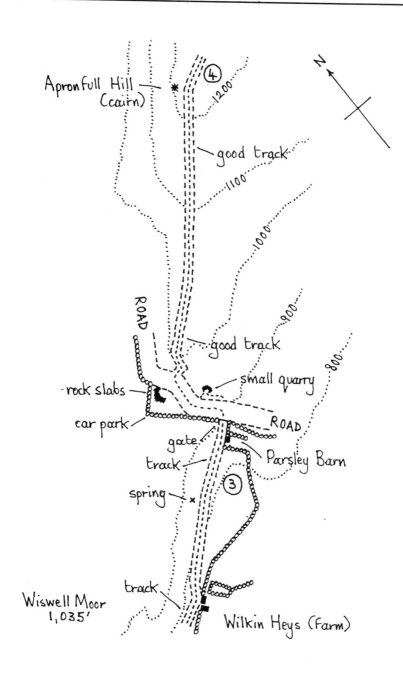

Apronfull Hill
(cairn)

④

1200

good track

1100

1000

900

ROAD

800

good track

small quarry

rock slabs

car park

ROAD

gate

Parsley Barn

track

spring

③

track

Wiswell Moor
1,035'

Wilkin Heys (Farm)

N

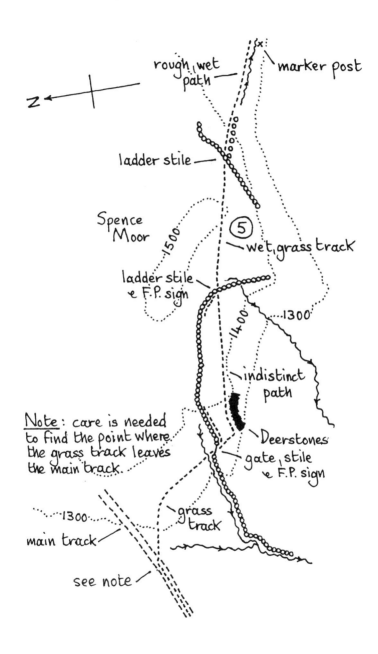

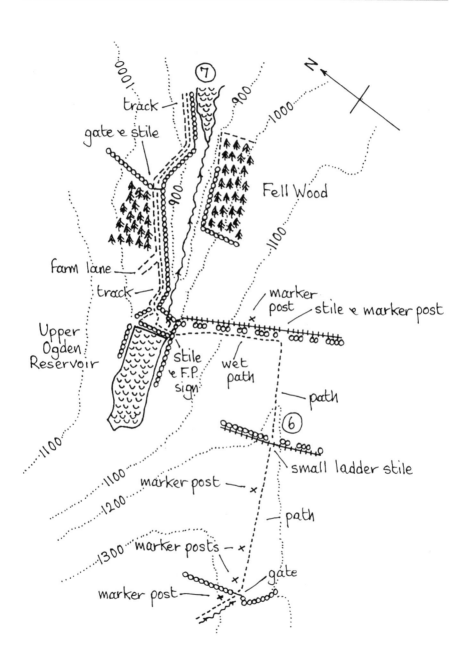

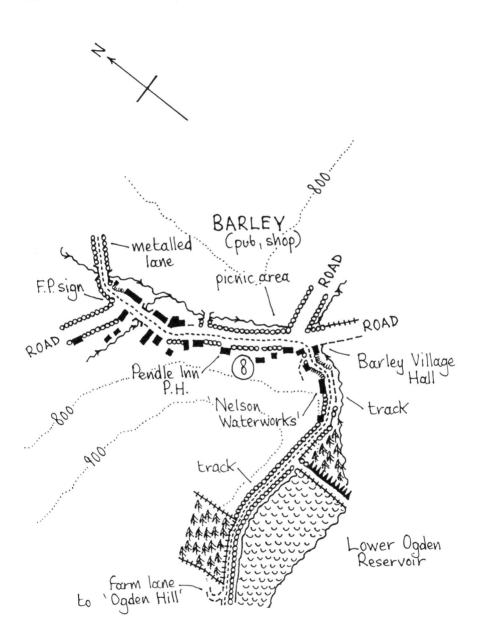

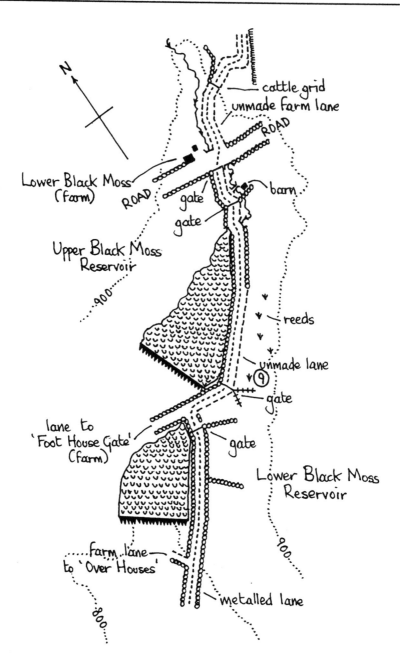

N

cattle grid
unmade farm lane
ROAD

Lower Black Moss
(farm)
ROAD
gate
gate
barn

Upper Black Moss
Reservoir
...900

reeds

unmade lane
⑨
gate

lane to
'Foot House Gate'
(farm)
gate

Lower Black Moss
Reservoir

farm lane
to 'Over Houses'
...800

metalled lane
...900

...800

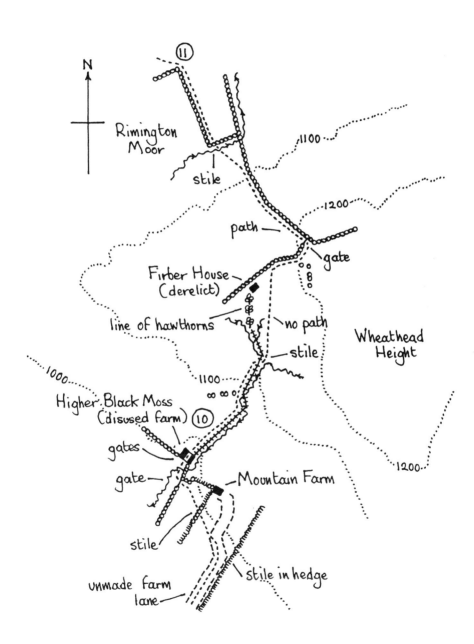

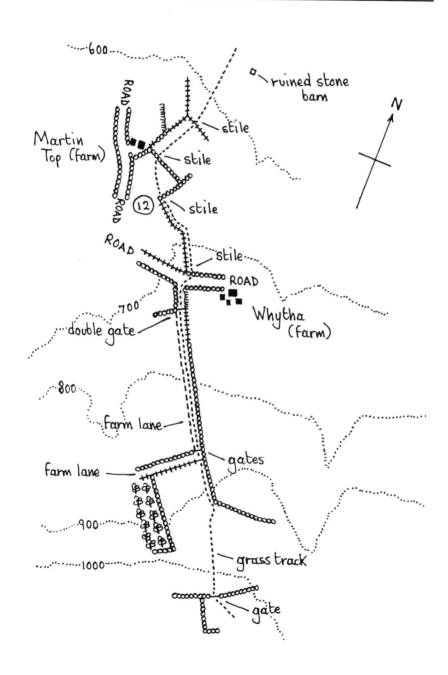

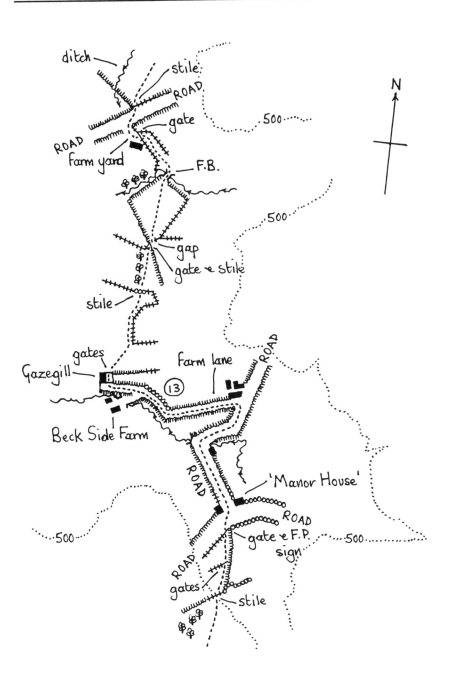

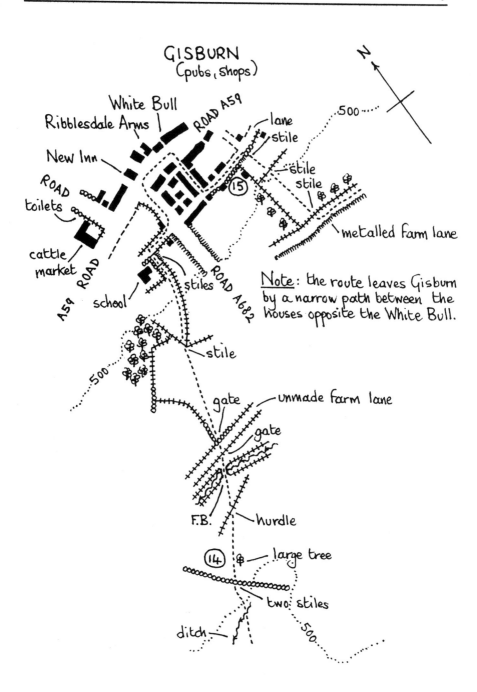

GISBURN
(pubs, shops)

White Bull
Ribblesdale Arms
ROAD A59

New Inn
ROAD
toilets

cattle
market
A59 ROAD
school

lane
stile
stile
stile

15

metalled farm lane

Note: the route leaves Gisburn
by a narrow path between the
houses opposite the White Bull.

stiles
ROAD A682

500
stile

gate — unmade farm lane

gate

F.B.   hurdle

14   large tree

two stiles

ditch   500

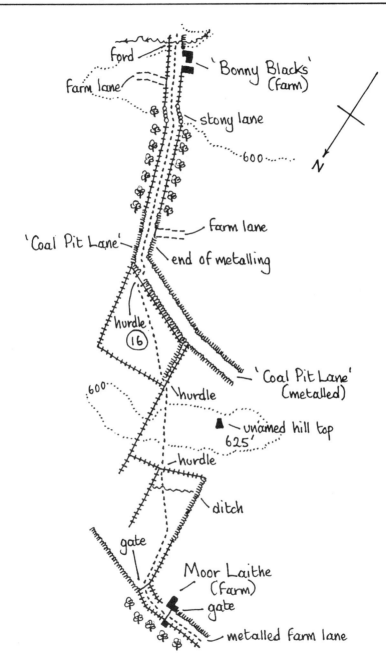

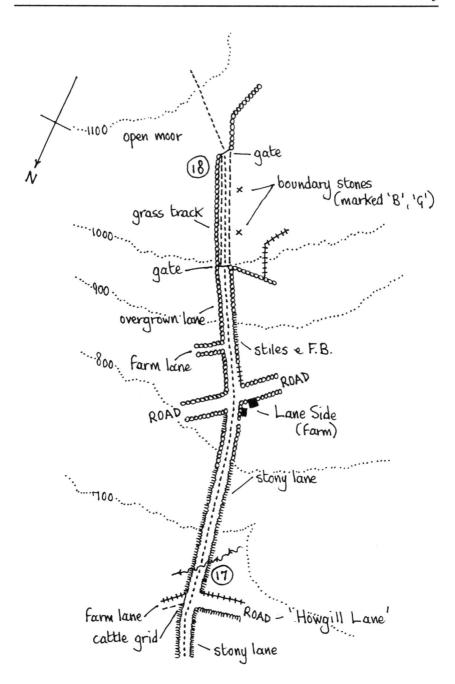

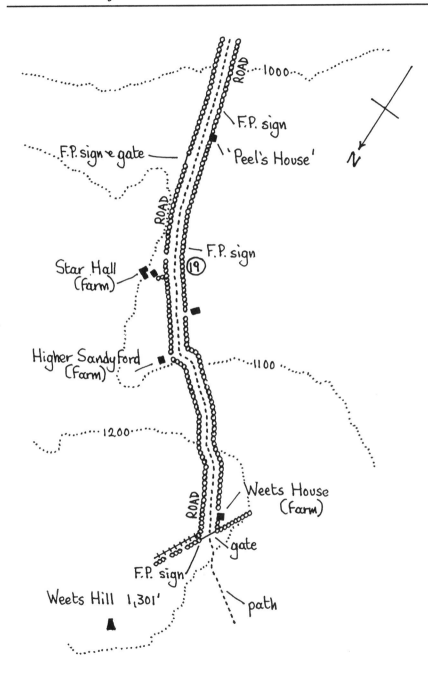

ROAD

····1000····

F.P. sign

F.P. sign & gate

'Peel's House'

N

ROAD

F.P. sign

⑲

Star Hall
(Farm)

Higher Sandyford
(Farm)

····1100····

····1200····

ROAD

Weets House
(Farm)

gate

F.P. sign

path

Weets Hill 1,301'

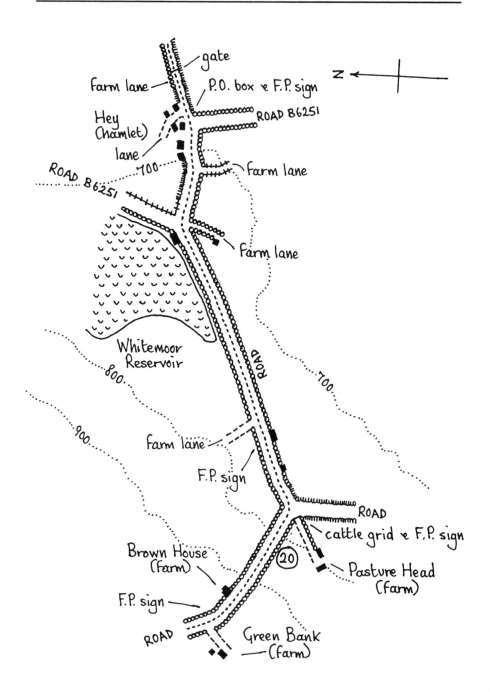

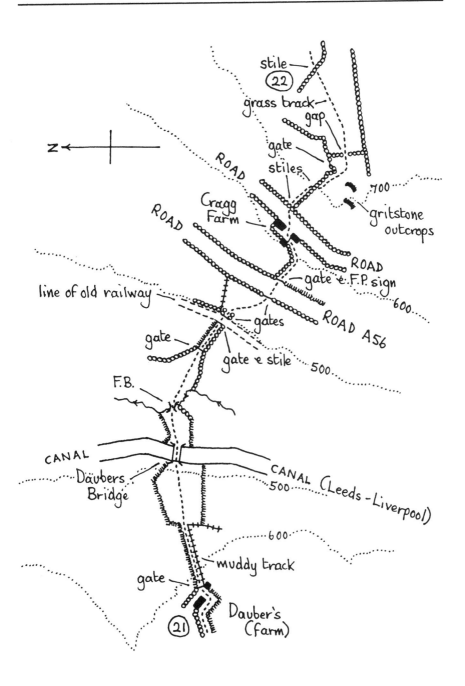

stile
(22)
grass track
gap
gate
stiles
gritstone outcrops
700
ROAD
Cragg Farm
ROAD
ROAD
gate & F.P. sign
600
line of old railway
ROAD A56
gates
gate
gate & stile
500
F.B.
CANAL
CANAL (Leeds-Liverpool)
Daubers Bridge
500
600
muddy track
gate
Dauber's (farm)
(21)

Z

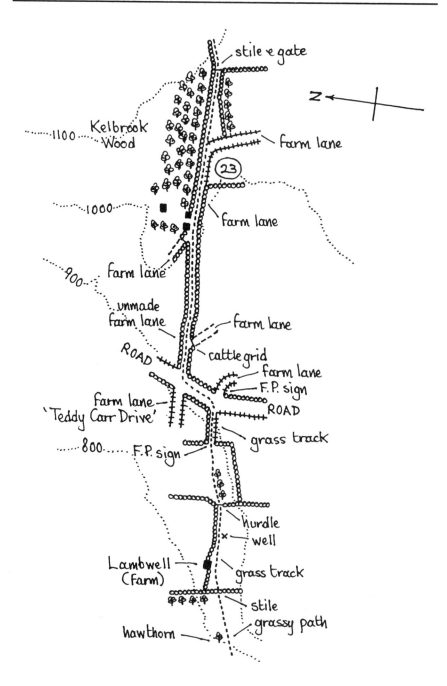

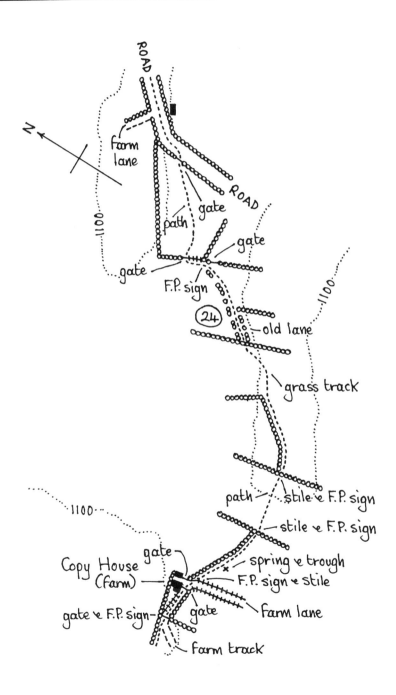

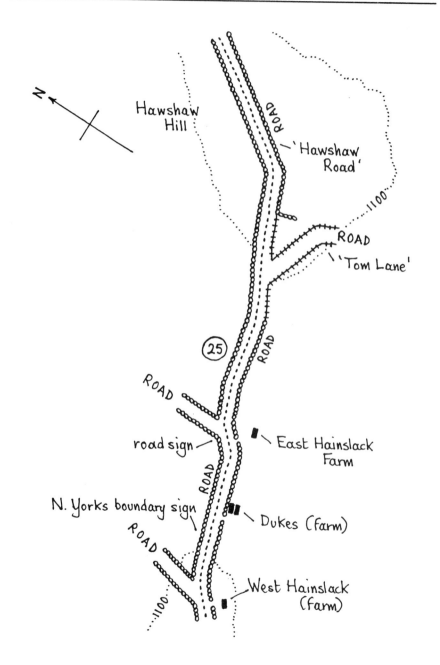

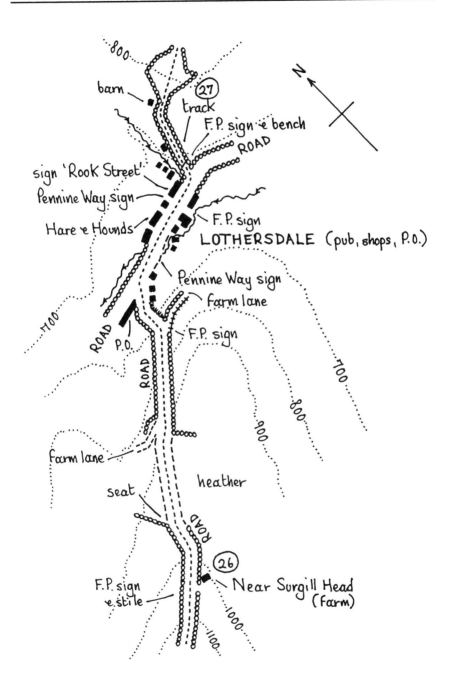

800

barn

27

track

F.P. sign ε bench

ROAD

N

sign 'Rook Street'

Pennine Way sign

Hare ε Hounds

F.P. sign

LOTHERSDALE (pub, shops, P.O.)

Pennine Way sign

farm lane

700

ROAD

P.O.

F.P. sign

ROAD

700

800

900

farm lane

heather

seat

ROAD

F.P. sign
ε stile

26

Near Surgill Head
(Farm)

1000

1100

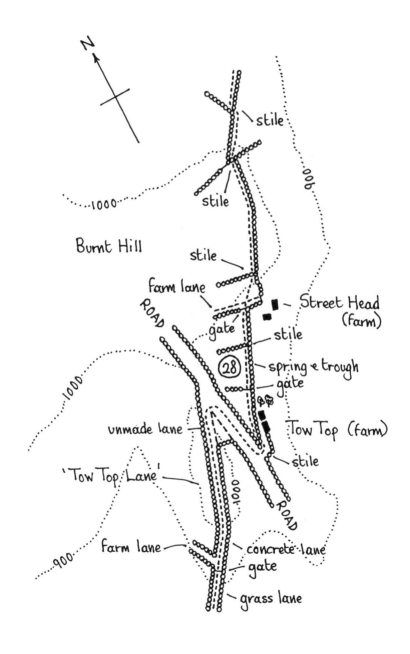

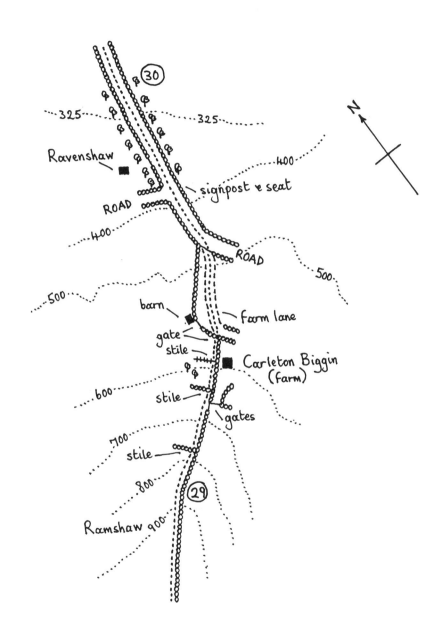

30

325 · · · 325 · · ·

Ravenshaw

400 · · ·

signpost & seat

ROAD

400 · · ·

ROAD

500 · · ·

500 · · ·

barn

farm lane

gate

stile

Carleton Biggin
(farm)

600 · · ·

stile

stile

gates

700 · · ·

stile

800 · · ·

29

Ramshaw 900 · · ·

N

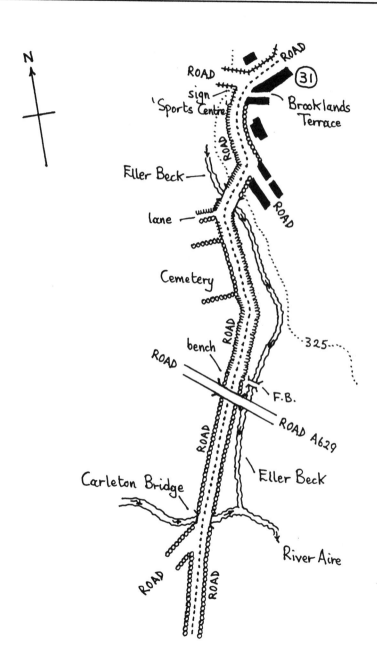

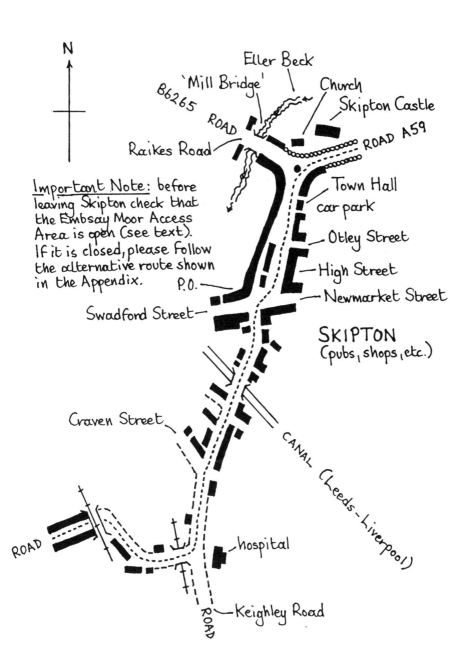

N

Eller Beck

'Mill Bridge'

Church

Skipton Castle

B6265 ROAD

ROAD A59

Raikes Road

Town Hall

car park

Important Note: before
leaving Skipton check that
the Embsay Moor Access
Area is open (see text).
If it is closed, please follow
the alternative route shown
in the Appendix.

Otley Street

High Street

P.O.

Newmarket Street

Swadford Street

SKIPTON
(pubs, shops, etc.)

Craven Street

CANAL (Leeds - Liverpool)

ROAD

hospital

ROAD

Keighley Road

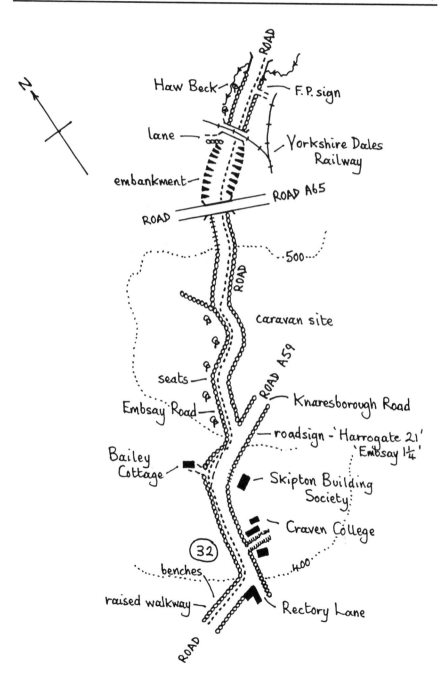

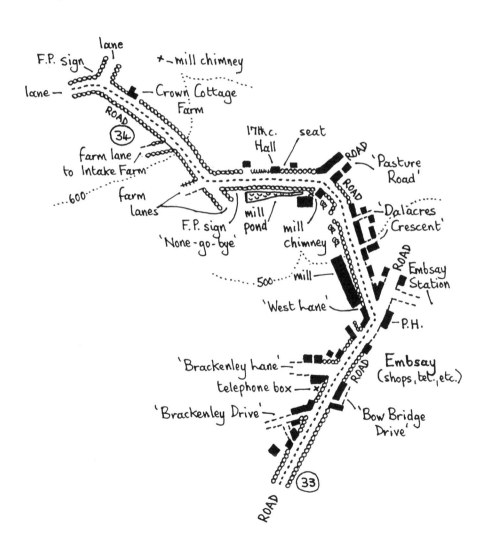

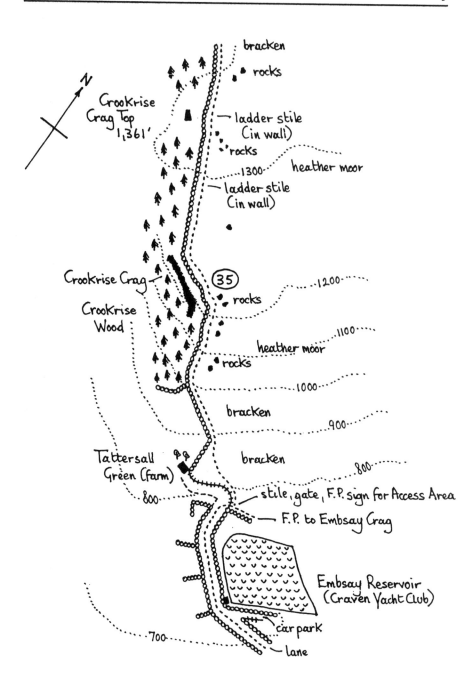

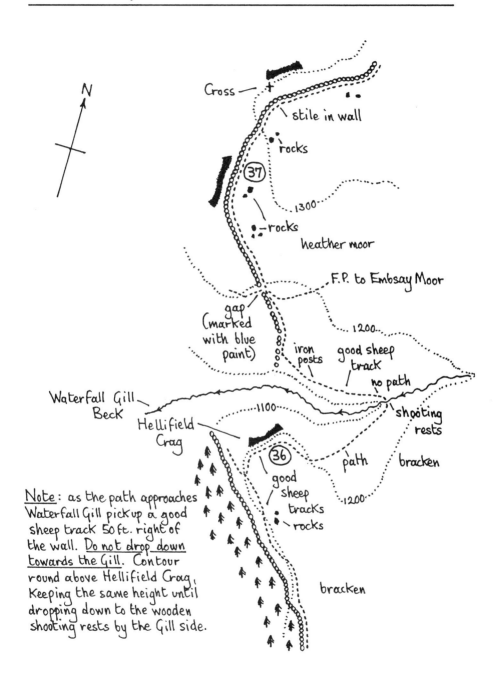

N

Cross — ✝

stile in wall

rocks

③⑦

...1300...

—rocks

heather moor

F.P. to Embsay Moor

gap
(marked
with blue
paint)

iron
posts

...1200...

good sheep
track

no path

Waterfall Gill
Beck

Hellifield
Crag

③⑥

...1100...

shooting
rests

good
sheep
tracks

path

bracken

—rocks

Note: as the path approaches
Waterfall Gill pick up a good
sheep track 50 ft. right of
the wall. Do not drop down
towards the Gill. Contour
round above Hellifield Crag,
Keeping the same height until
dropping down to the wooden
shooting rests by the Gill side.

...1200...

bracken

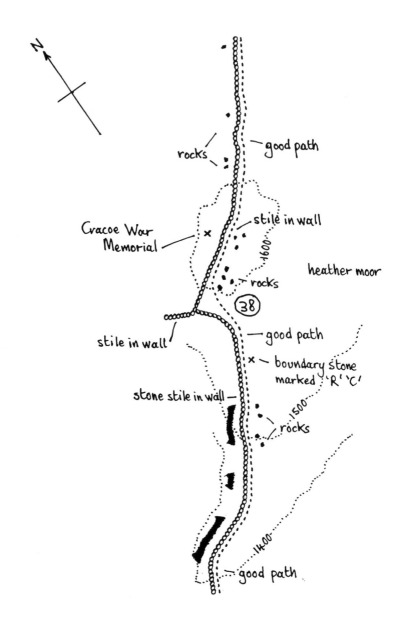

N

rocks — good path

Cracoe War
Memorial

stile in wall

1600

heather moor

rocks

38

stile in wall — good path

x — boundary stone
marked 'R' 'C'

stone stile in wall —

1500

rocks

1400

good path

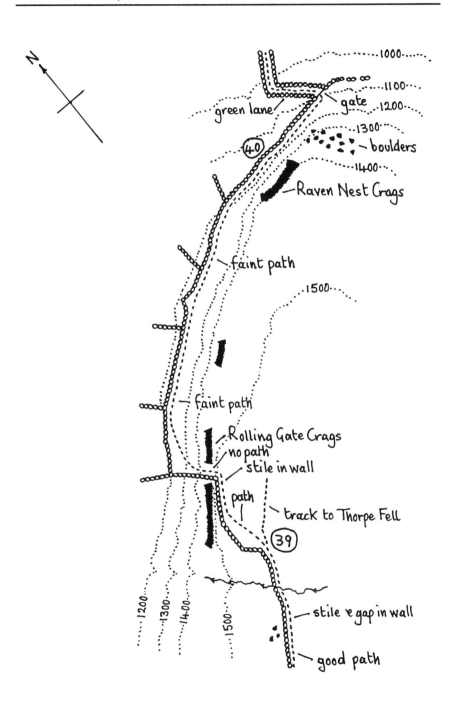

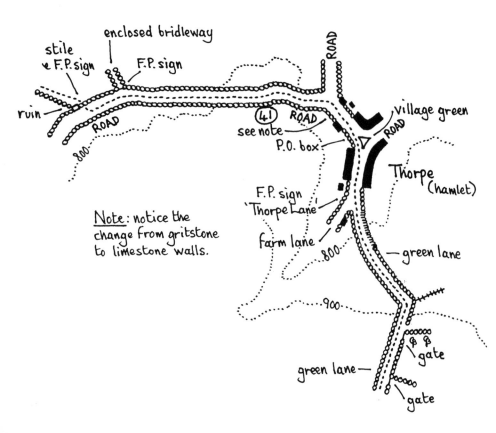

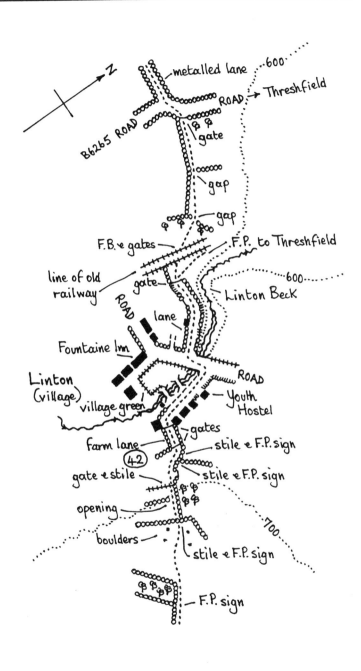

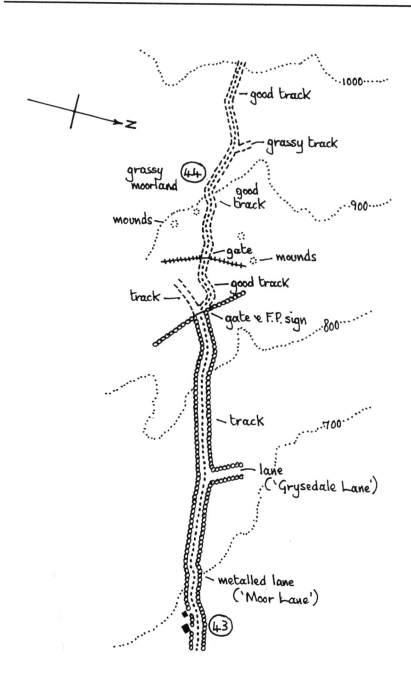

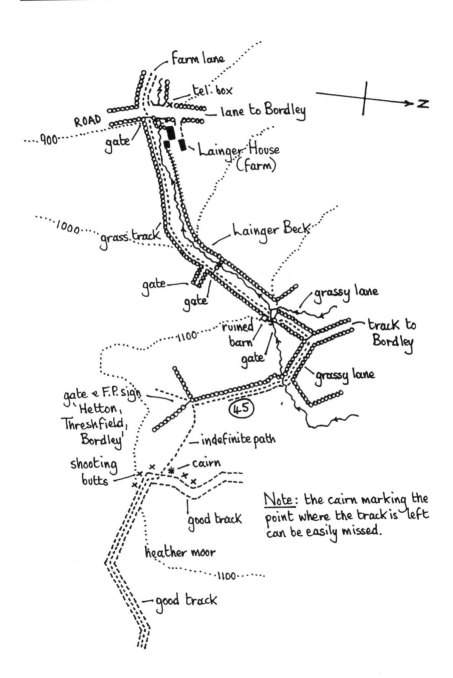

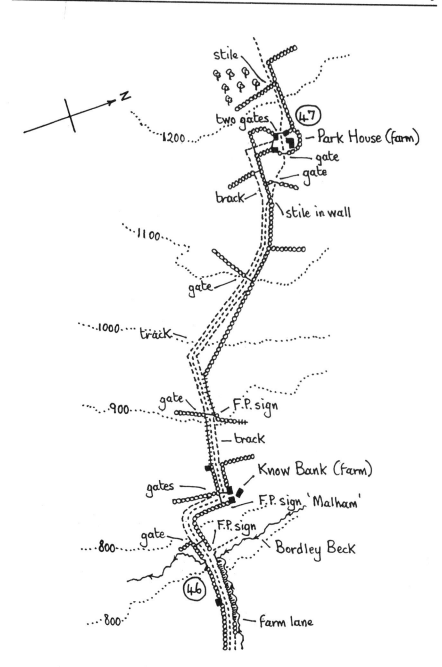

stile

Z

two gates   47
                        — Park House (farm)
1200   gate
                            gate
        track
                    stile in wall

1100

    gate

1000   track

    gate   F.P. sign
900
                    track

                    Know Bank (farm)
gates
                    F.P. sign 'Malham'

            F.P. sign
gate
800   Bordley Beck

        46

800   farm lane

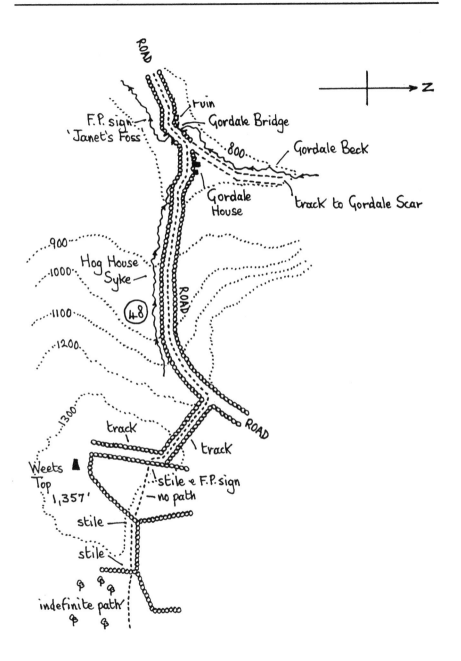

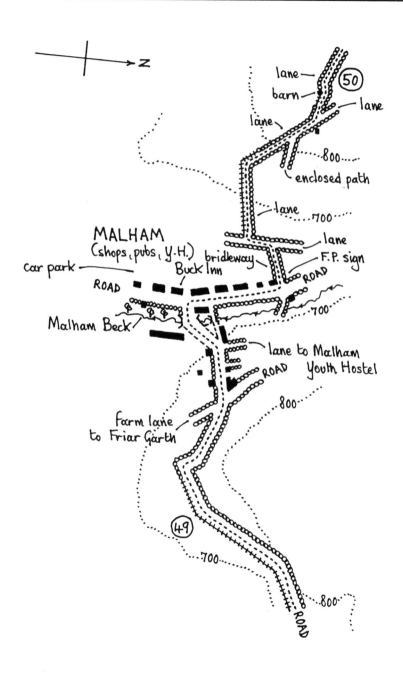

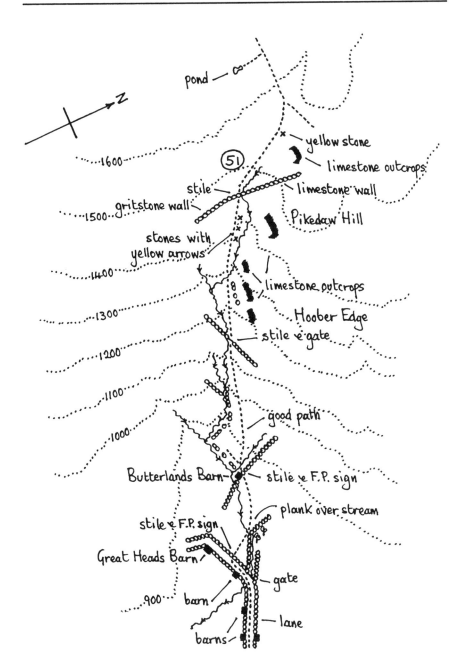

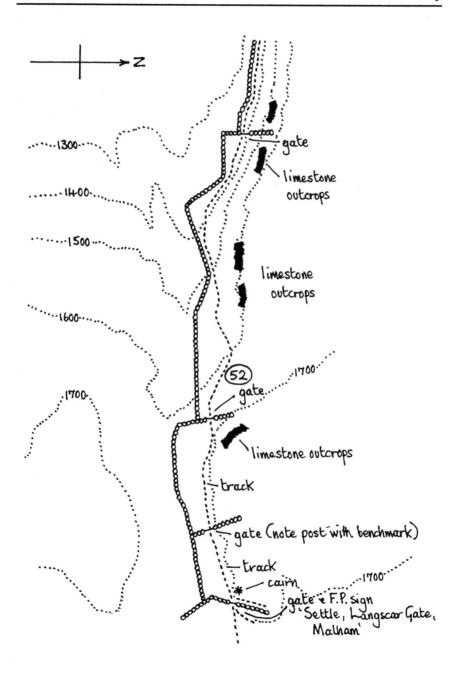

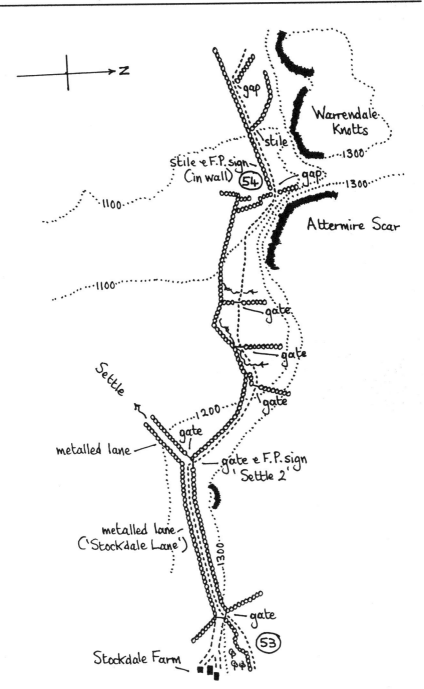

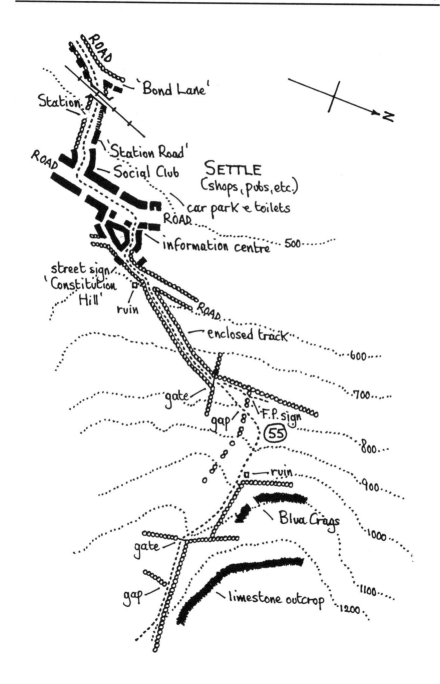

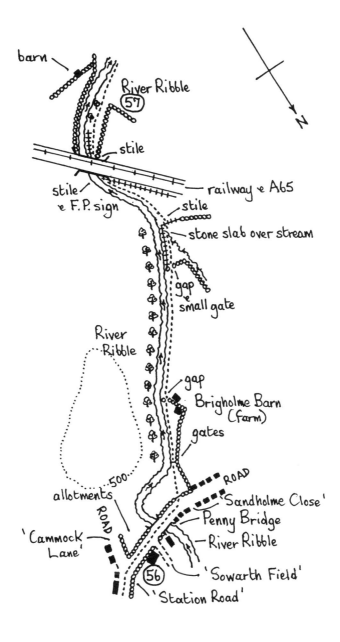

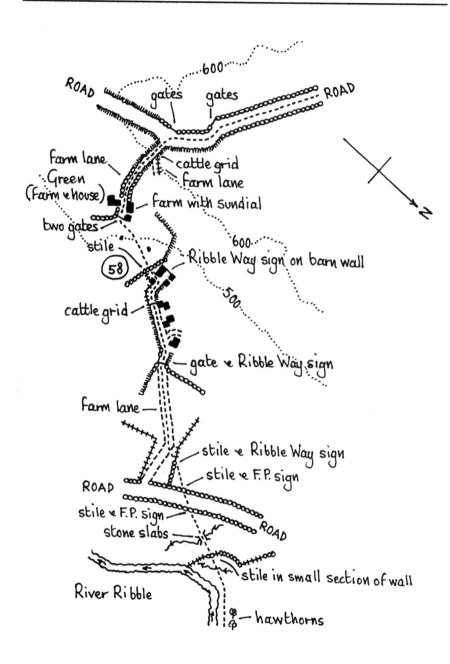

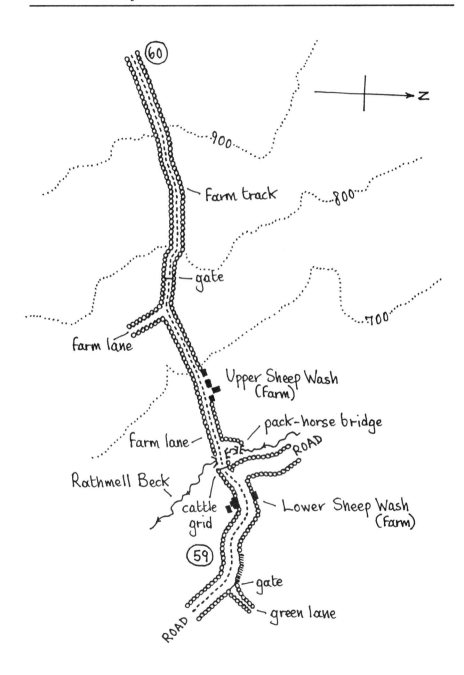

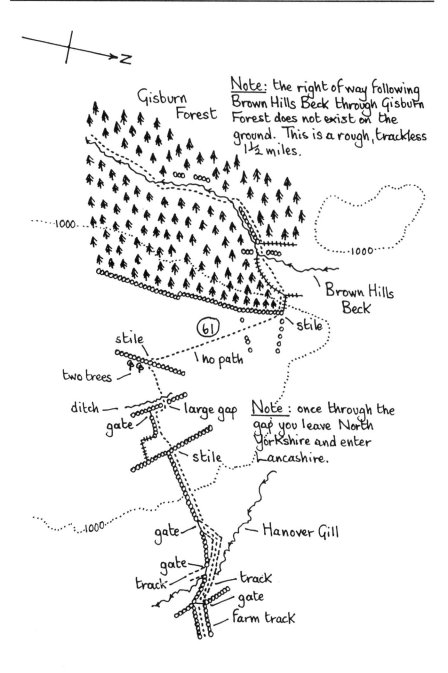

Gisburn Forest

Note: the right of way following Brown Hills Beck through Gisburn Forest does not exist on the ground. This is a rough, trackless 1½ miles.

1000

1000

Brown Hills Beck

61

stile

stile

no path

two trees

ditch — large gap

gate

Note: once through the gap you leave North Yorkshire and enter Lancashire.

stile

1000

gate — Hanover Gill

gate

track — track

gate

farm track

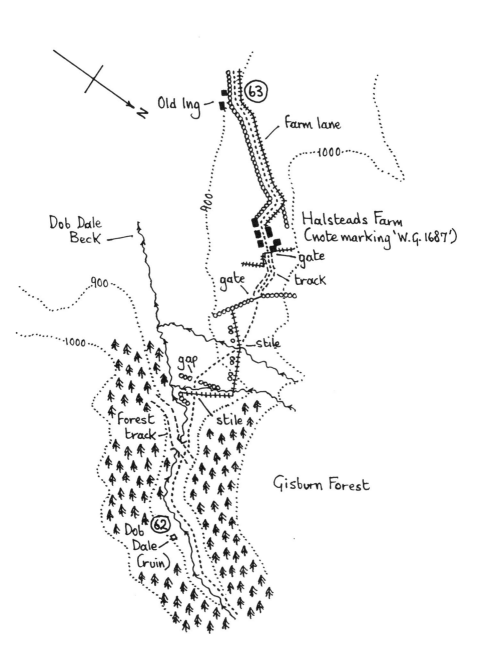

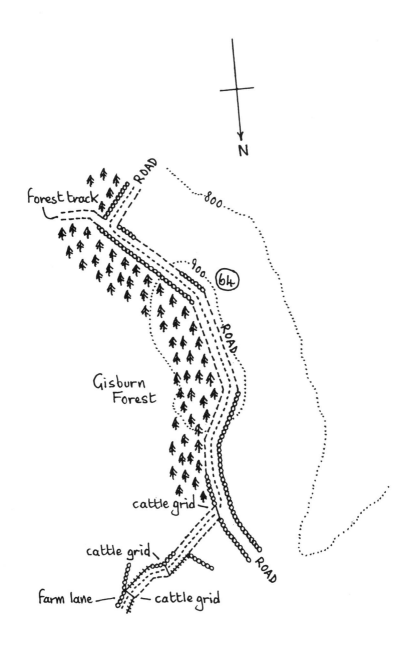

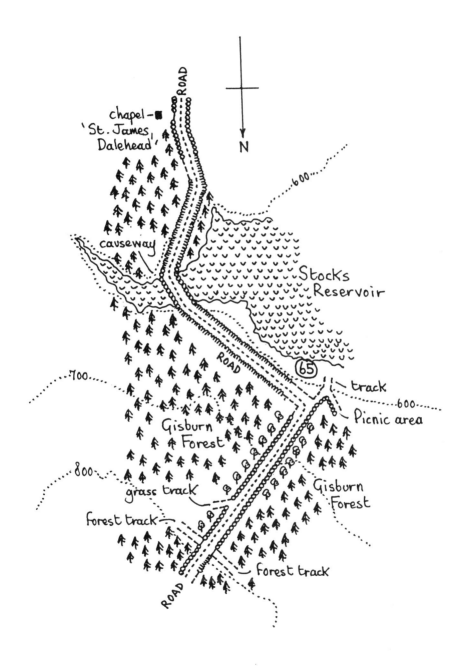

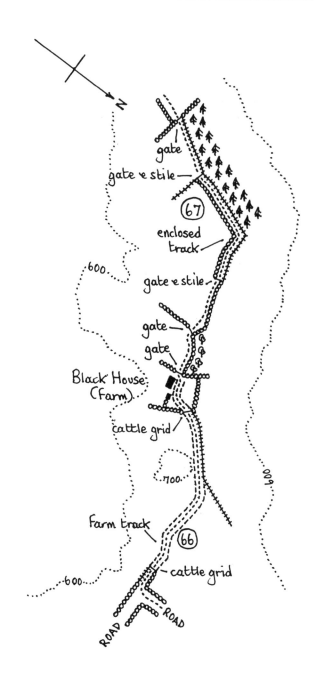

N

gate

gate & stile —

67

enclosed
track

·600·

gate & stile

gate —

gate

Black House
(Farm)

cattle grid

·700·

Farm track

66

·600·

cattle grid

ROAD

ROAD

·600·

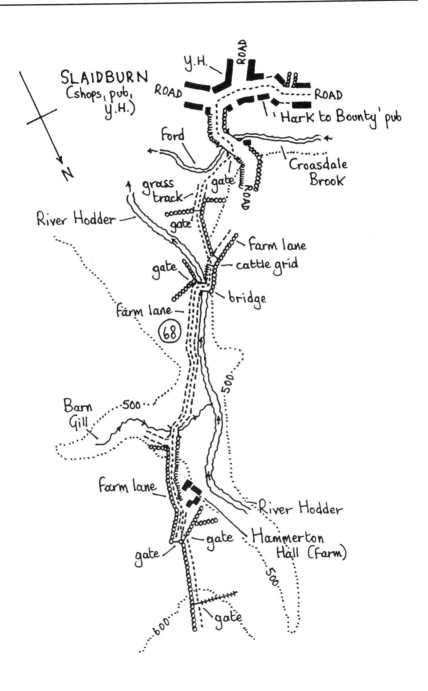

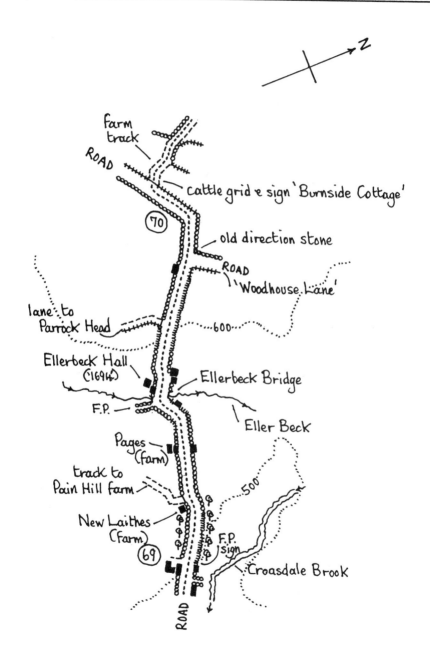

Z

farm
track

ROAD

cattle grid e sign 'Burnside Cottage'

70

old direction stone

ROAD
'Woodhouse Lane'

lane to
Parrock Head

600

Ellerbeck Hall
(1694)

Ellerbeck Bridge

F.P.

Eller Beck

Pages
(farm)

track to
Pain Hill farm

500

New Laithes
(farm)

69

F.P.
Sign

Croasdale Brook

ROAD

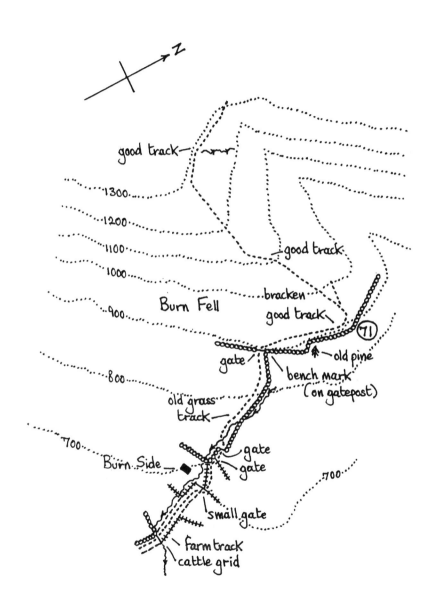

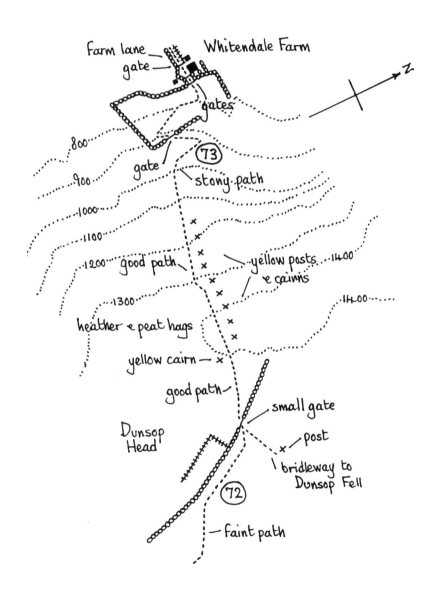

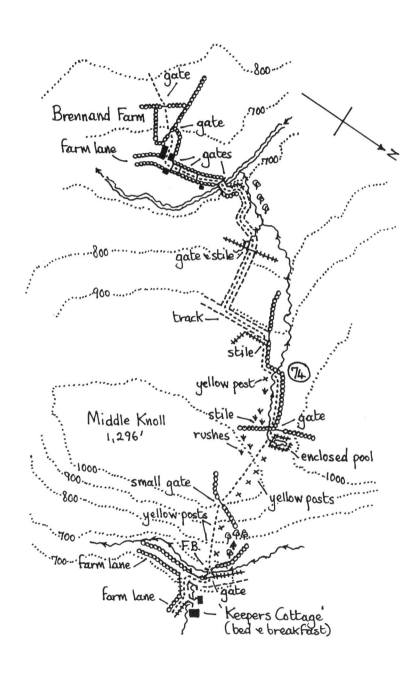

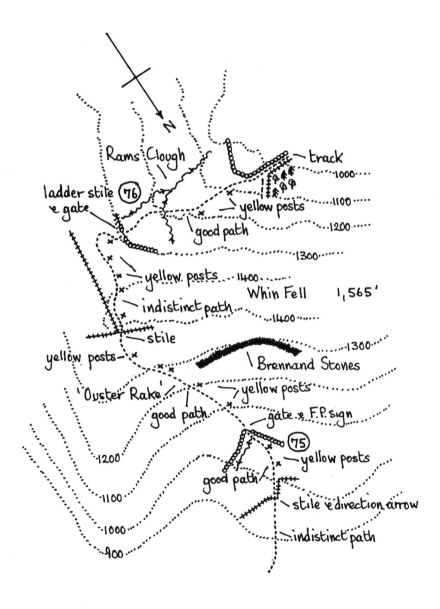

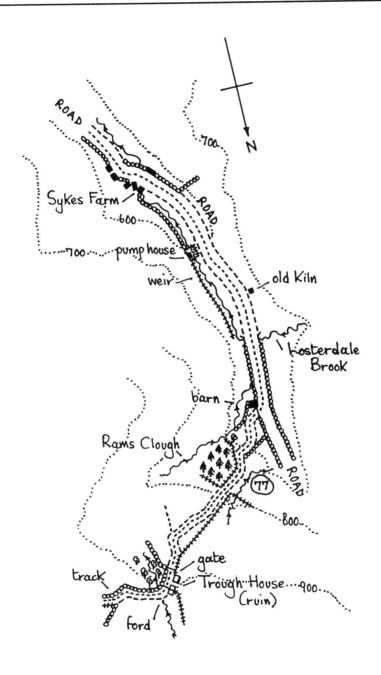

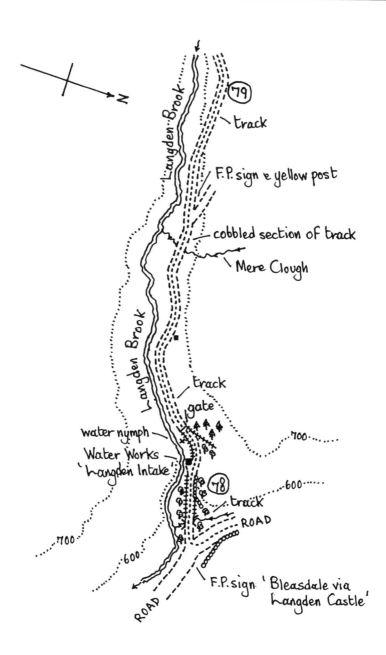

N

Langden·Brook

79
track

F.P. sign & yellow post

cobbled section of track

Mere Clough

Langden Brook

track

gate

water nymph
Water Works
'Langden Intake'

700

78
600

track

ROAD

700

600

ROAD

F.P. sign 'Bleasdale via
Langden Castle'

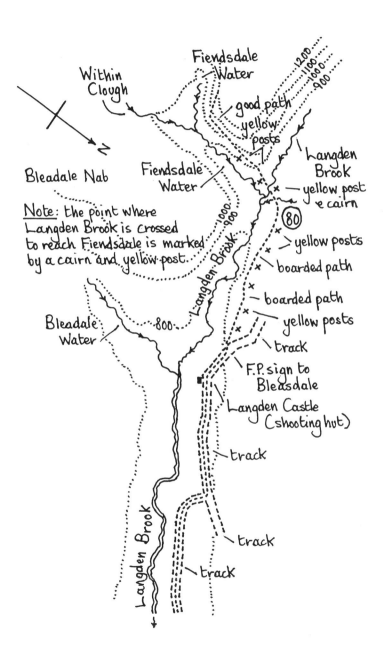

Within Clough

Fiendsdale Water

good path

yellow posts

Langden Brook

Bleadale Nab

Fiendsdale Water

yellow post & cairn

80

Note: the point where Langden Brook is crossed to reach Fiendsdale is marked by a cairn and yellow post.

yellow posts

boarded path

boarded path

yellow posts

Bleadale Water

800

track

F.P. sign to Bleasdale

Langden Castle (shooting hut)

track

Langden Brook

track

track

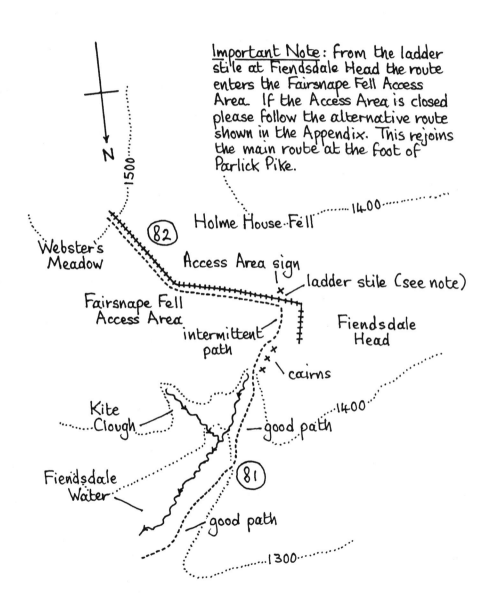

Important Note: From the ladder stile at Fiendsdale Head the route enters the Fairsnape Fell Access Area. If the Access Area is closed please follow the alternative route shown in the Appendix. This rejoins the main route at the foot of Parlick Pike.

N

1500

Webster's Meadow

82

Holme House Fell

1400

Access Area sign

ladder stile (see note)

×

Fairsnape Fell Access Area

Fiendsdale Head

intermittent path

×
×
×

cairns

Kite Clough

1400

good path

Fiendsdale Water

81

good path

1300

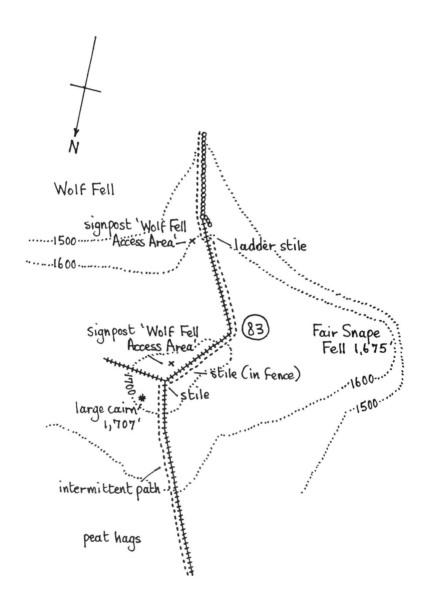

N

Wolf Fell

signpost 'Wolf Fell
Access Area'   × ladder stile
······1500·······
·····1600·····

Signpost 'Wolf Fell   83   Fair Snape
Access Area'   Fell 1,675'
              ×   stile (in fence)   1600·····
1700   ·1500·····
large cairn   stile
      1,707'

intermittent path

peat hags

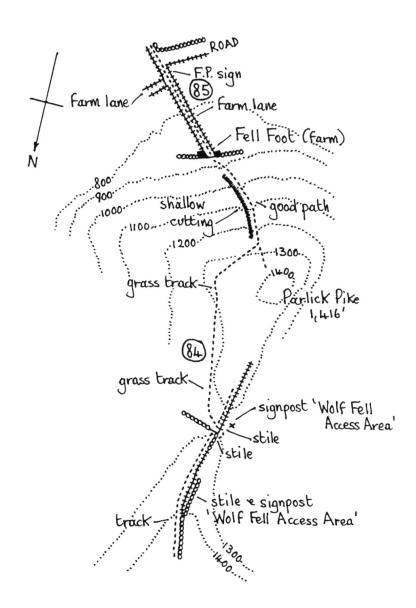

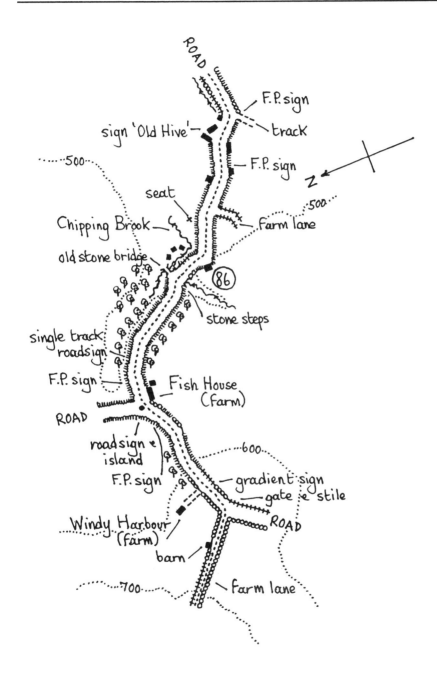

ROAD

F.P. sign

track

sign 'Old Hive'

F.P. sign

500

seat

Chipping Brook

Z

500

Farm lane

old stone bridge

86

stone steps

single track roadsign

F.P. sign

Fish House (Farm)

ROAD

roadsign & island

600

F.P. sign

gradient sign

gate & stile

Windy Harbour (Farm)

ROAD

barn

700

Farm lane

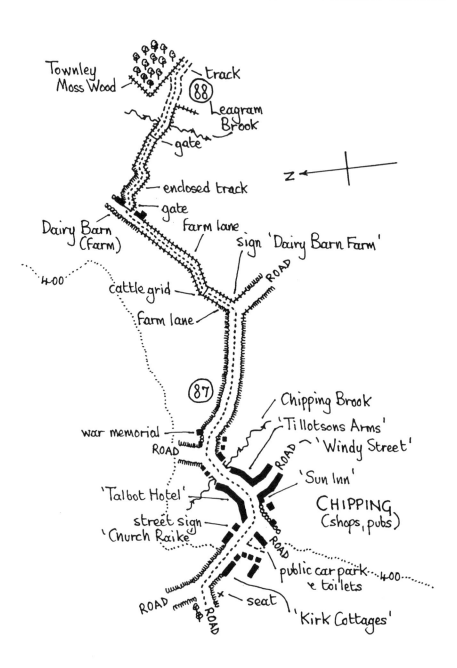

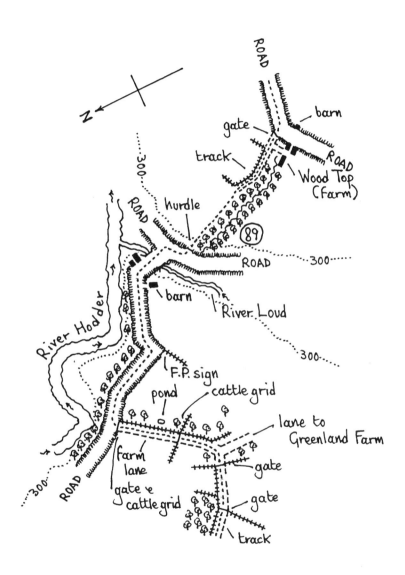

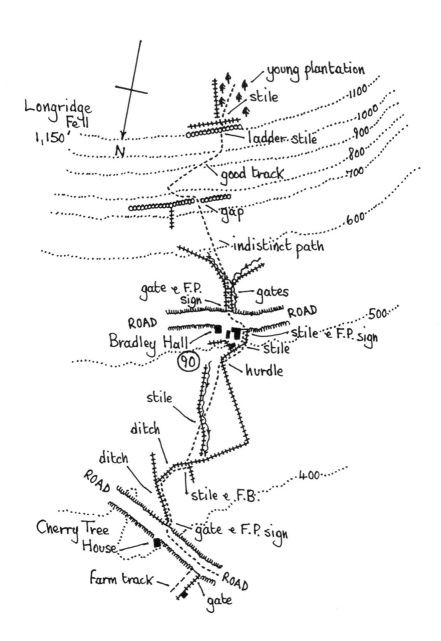

young plantation

stile

Longridge
Fell
1,150'

N

1100

1000

900

ladder stile

good track

800

700

gap

600

indistinct path

gate & F.P.
sign

gates

ROAD

ROAD

500

stile & F.P. sign

ROAD

Bradley Hall

stile

90

stile

hurdle

stile

ditch

ditch

ROAD

400

stile & F.B.

gate & F.P. sign

Cherry Tree
House

farm track

ROAD

gate

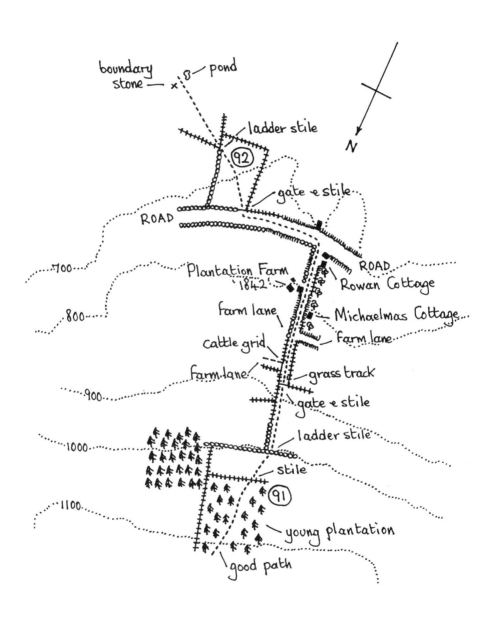

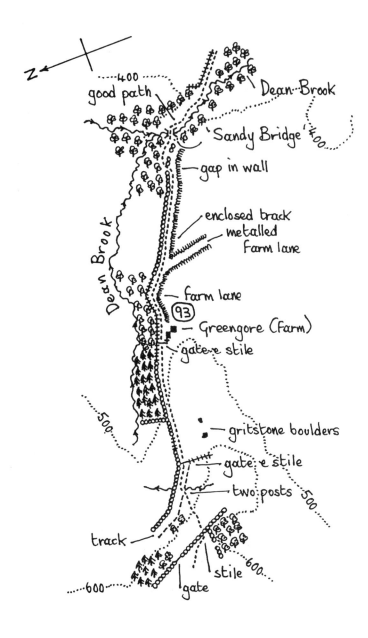

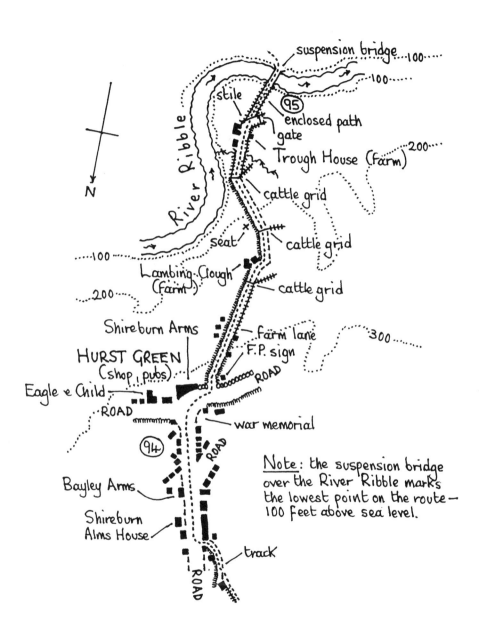

Note: the suspension bridge over the River Ribble marks the lowest point on the route — 100 feet above sea level.

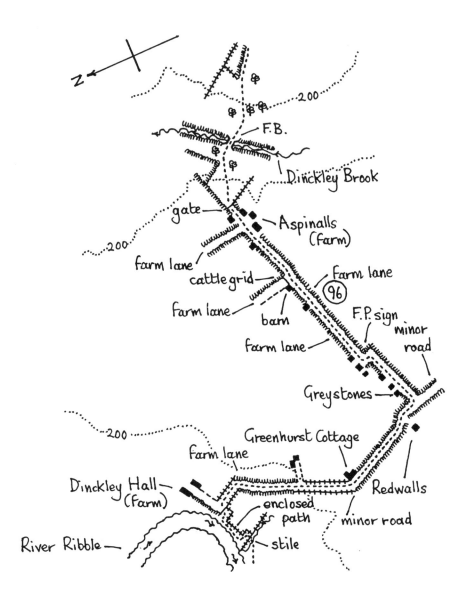

Z

200

F.B.

Dinckley Brook

gate

Aspinalls (Farm)

200

farm lane

cattle grid

Farm lane (96)

farm lane

barn

F.P. sign

minor road

farm lane

Greystones

200

Greenhurst Cottage

Farm lane

Dinckley Hall (Farm)

Redwalls

enclosed path

minor road

River Ribble

stile

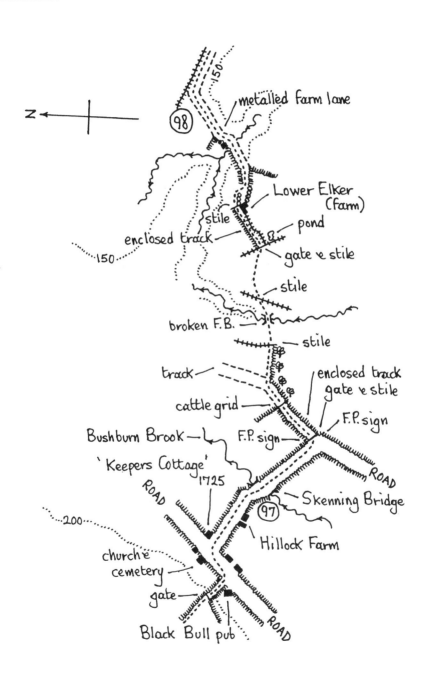

N ←

metalled farm lane

98

Lower Elker
(farm)

stile

enclosed track

pond

gate & stile

150

stile

broken F.B.

stile

track

enclosed track
gate & stile

cattle grid

F.P. sign

Bushburn Brook

F.P. sign

'Keepers Cottage'
1725

ROAD

ROAD

Skenning Bridge

97

200

Hillock Farm

church &
cemetery

gate

Black Bull pub

ROAD

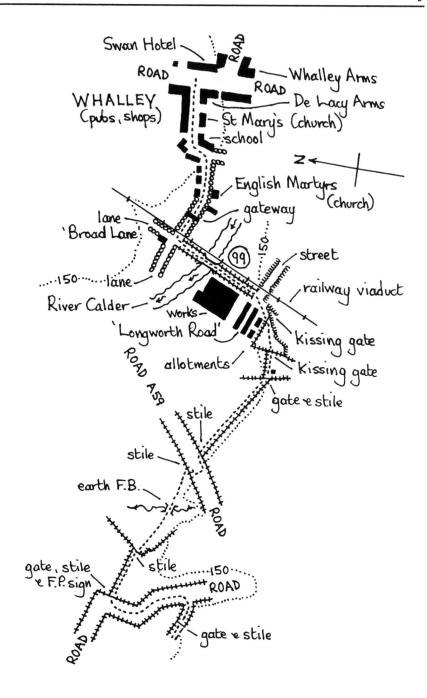

Appendix: Alternative Route Maps

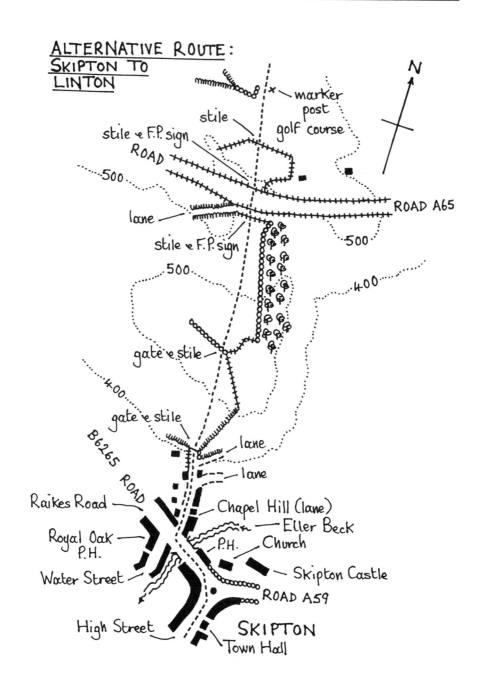

ALTERNATIVE ROUTE:
SKIPTON TO
LINTON

N

marker post

stile

golf course

stile & F.P. sign

ROAD

500

ROAD A65

lane

stile & F.P. sign

500

500

400

gate & stile

400

gate & stile

B6265 ROAD

lane

lane

Raikes Road

Chapel Hill (lane)

Eller Beck

Royal Oak P.H.

P.H.

Church

Water Street

Skipton Castle

ROAD A59

High Street

SKIPTON
Town Hall

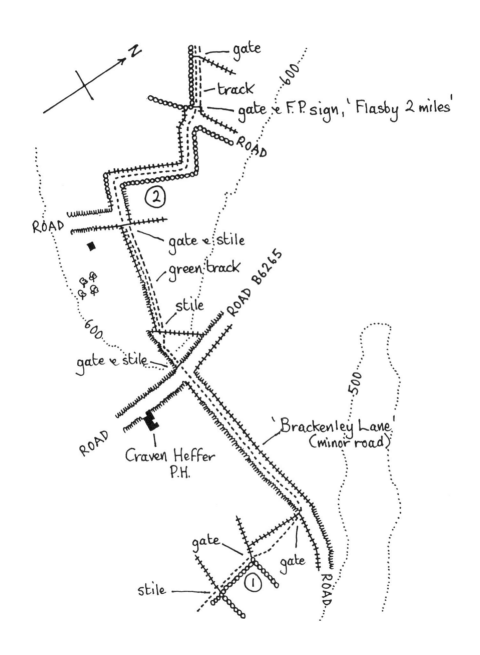

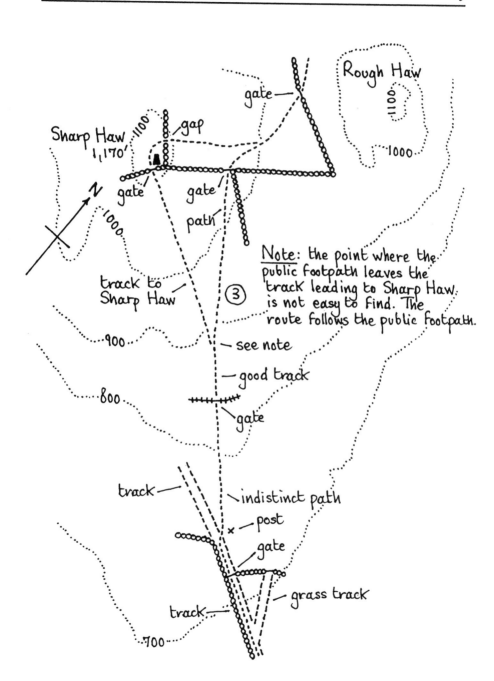

Rough Haw

1100

1000

gate

Sharp Haw
1,170'   gap

N

1000

gate   gate

path

Note: the point where the public footpath leaves the track leading to Sharp Haw is not easy to find. The route follows the public footpath.

track to
Sharp Haw

③

900

— see note

— good track

800

— gate

track —   \ indistinct path

× — post

gate

— grass track

track —

700

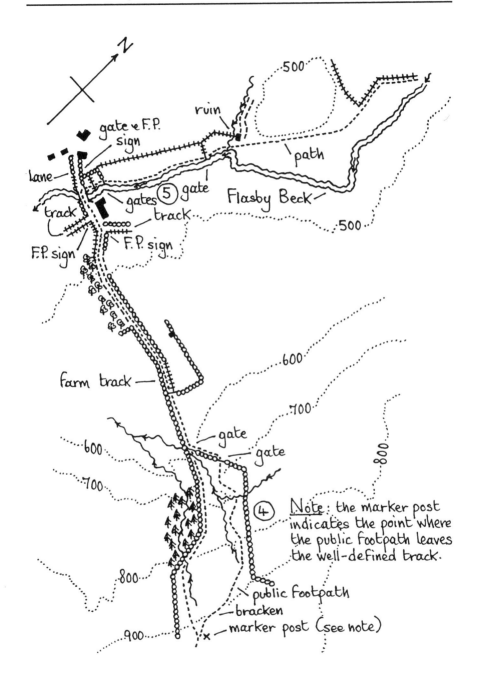

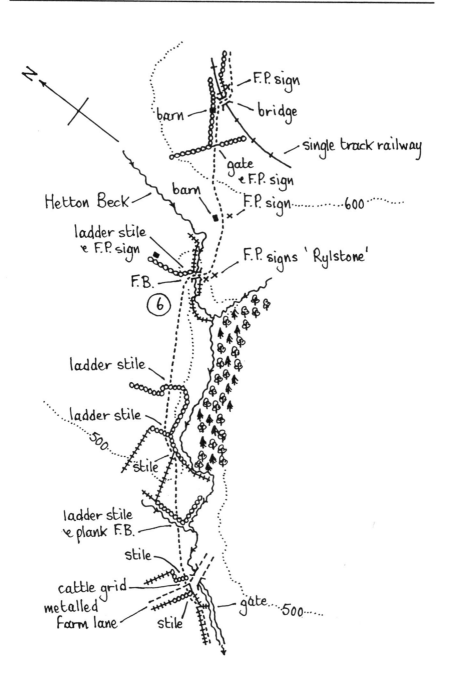

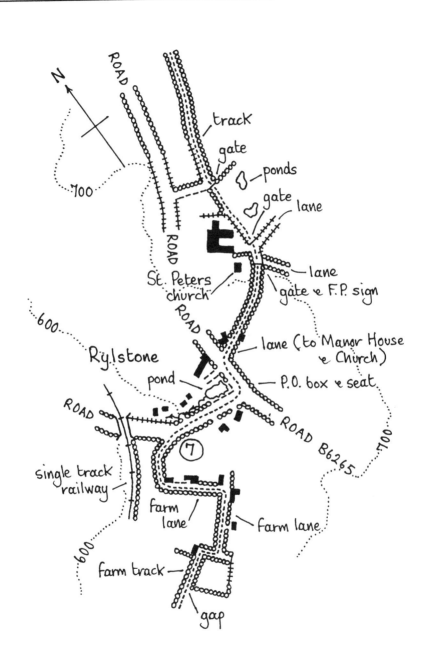

N

ROAD

track

gate

ponds

gate lane

ROAD

St. Peters
church

gate & F.P. sign

ROAD

700

600

Rylstone

pond

lane (to Manor House
& Church)

P.O. box & seat

ROAD

ROAD B6265

700

single track
railway

⑦

farm
lane

farm lane

600

farm track

gap

lane

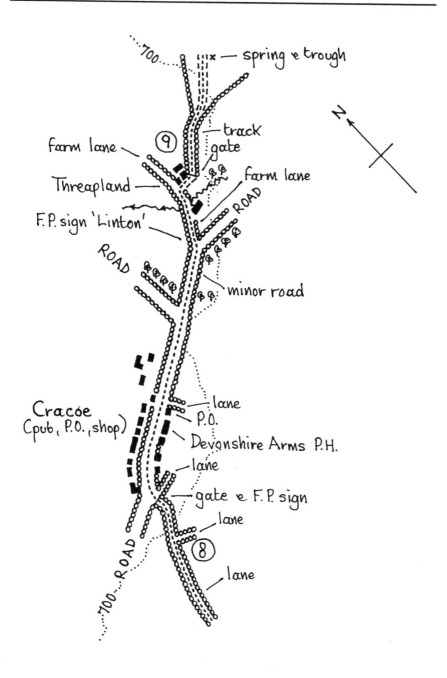

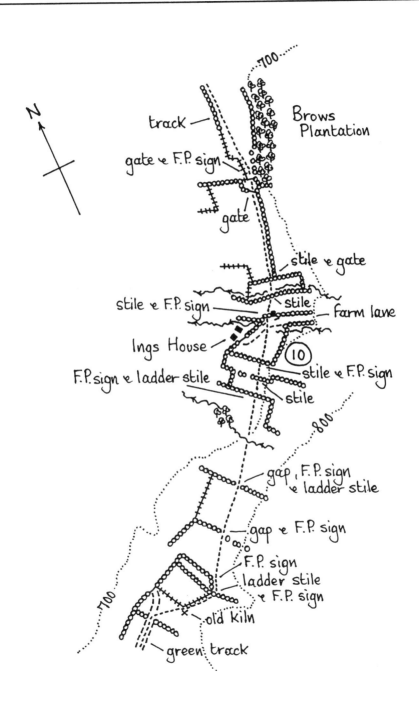

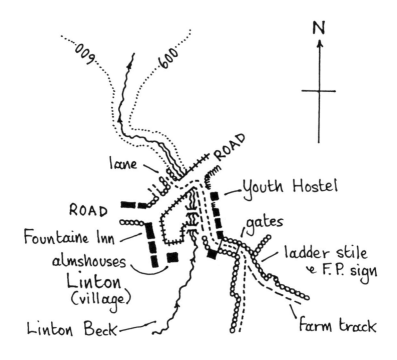

N

600

600

lane

ROAD

Youth Hostel

ROAD

gates

Fountaine Inn

almshouses

ladder stile
& F.P. sign

Linton
(village)

Linton Beck

farm track

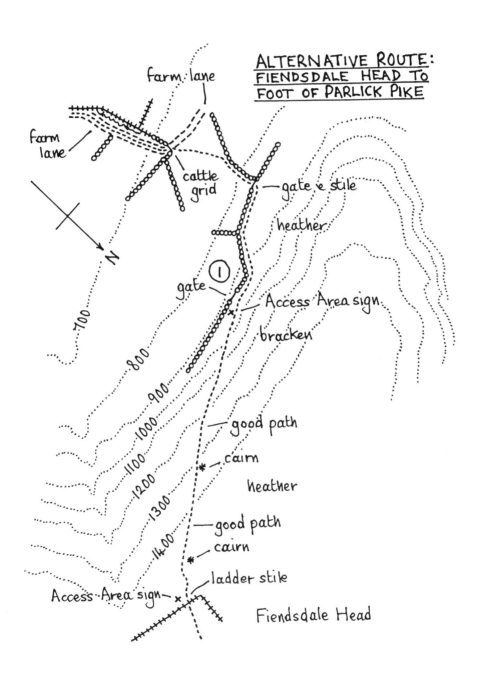

ALTERNATIVE ROUTE:
FIENDSDALE HEAD TO
FOOT OF PARLICK PIKE

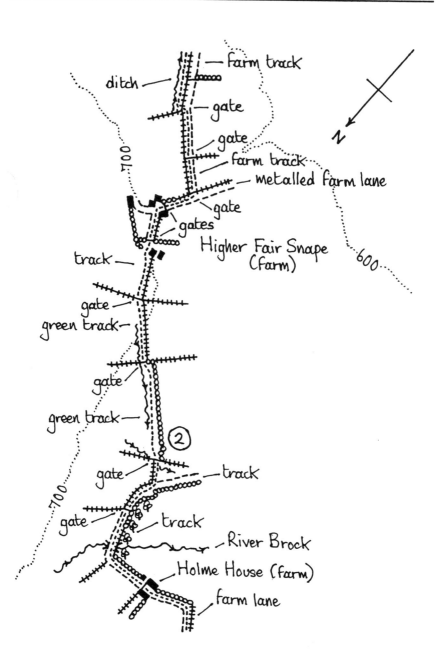

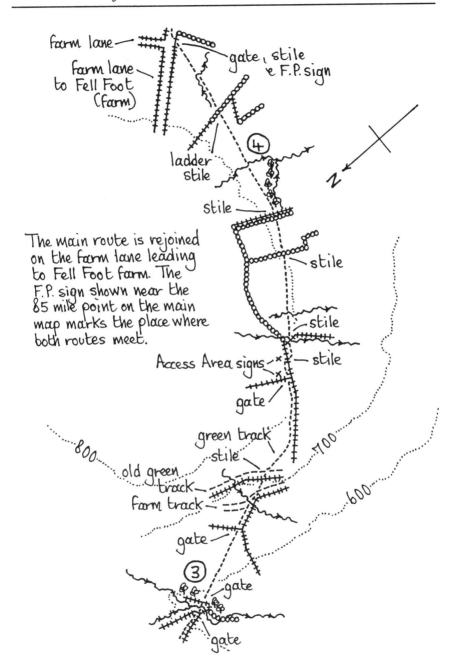

farm lane

farm lane to Fell Foot (farm)

gate, stile e F.P. sign

ladder stile

④

stile

The main route is rejoined on the farm lane leading to Fell Foot farm. The F.P. sign shown near the 85 mile point on the main map marks the place where both routes meet.

stile

stile

Access Area signs

stile

gate

green track

stile

800

old green track

700

Farm track

600

gate

③

gate

gate

Explore the countryside with Sigma!

We have a wide selection of guides to individual towns, plus outdoor activities centred on walking and cycling in the great outdoors throughout England and Wales. This is a recent selection:

Cycling with Sigma . . .

. . . just the start of our series of cycling books!

OFF-BEAT CYCLING & MOUNTAIN BIKING IN THE PEAK DISTRICT
– Clive Smith

MORE OFF-BEAT CYCLING IN THE PEAK DISTRICT
– Clive Smith

50 BEST CYCLE RIDES IN CHESHIRE
– edited by Graham Beech

BY-WAY TRAVELS SOUTH OF LONDON
– Geoff Marshall

BY-WAYS BIKING IN THE CHILTERNS

– Henry Tindell

General interest:

PEAK DISTRICT DIARY – Roger Redfern
An evocative book, celebrating the glorious countryside of the Peak District. The book is based on Roger's popular column in *The Guardian* newspaper and is profusely illustrated with stunning photographs. £6.95

I REMAIN, YOUR SON JACK – J. C. Morten (edited by Sheila Morten)
A collection of almost 200 letters, as featured on BBC TV, telling the moving story of a young soldier in the First World War. Profusely illustrated with contemporary photographs. £8.95

Books of Walks:

There are many books for outdoor people in our catalogue, including:

RAMBLES IN NORTH WALES
– Roger Redfern

HERITAGE WALKS IN THE PEAK DISTRICT
– Clive Price

EAST CHESHIRE WALKS
– Graham Beech

WEST CHESHIRE WALKS
– Jen Darling

WEST PENNINE WALKS
– Mike Cresswell

NEWARK AND SHERWOOD RAMBLES
– Malcolm McKenzie

RAMBLES AROUND NOTTINGHAM & DERBY
– Keith Taylor

RAMBLES AROUND MANCHESTER
– Mike Cresswell

WESTERN LAKELAND RAMBLES
– Gordon Brown

WELSH WALKS:
Dolgellau and the Cambrian Coast
– Laurence Main and Morag Perrott

WELSH WALKS:
Aberystwyth and District
– Laurence Main and Morag Perrott

– all of these books are currently £6.95 each.

Long-distance walks:

THE STAFFORDSHIRE WAY
Les Lumsdon and Chris Rushton

THE GREATER MANCHESTER BOUNDARY WALK
– Graham Phythian

THE THIRLMERE WAY
– Tim Cappelli

THE FURNESS TRAIL
– Tim Cappelli

THE MARCHES WAY
– Les Lumsdon

– all £6.95 each

We also publish:

Guidebooks to the smaller breweries to the 'Pubs of Old Lancashire'

**A fabulous series of 'Pub Walks' books for just about
every popular walking area in the UK,
all featuring access by public transport**

**A new series of investigations into the Supernatural,
Myth and Magic**

Superb illustrated books on Manchester's football teams

– plus many more entertaing and educational books being regularly added to
our list.

All of our books are available from your local bookshop. In case of difficulty, or
to obtain our complete catalogue, please contact:

Sigma Leisure,

1 South Oak Lane,

Wilmslow, Cheshire SK9 6AR

Phone: 0625 – 531035 Fax: 0625 – 536800

ACCESS and VISA orders welcome – call our friendly sales staff or use our 24
hour Answerphone service! Most orders are despatched on the day we receive
your order – you could be enjoying our books in just a couple of days.